GLACIER NATIONAL PARK AND WATERTON LAKES NATIONAL PARK

A COMPLETE RECREATION GUIDE

VICKY SPRING

PHOTOS BY
VICKY SPRING AND TOM KIRKENDALL

THE
MOUNTAINEERS

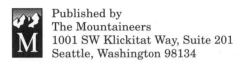
Published by
The Mountaineers
1001 SW Klickitat Way, Suite 201
Seattle, Washington 98134

Published simultaneously in Canada by Rocky Mountain Books, #4 Spruce
Centre SW, Calgary, AB, Canada, T3C 3B3

Published simultaneously in Great Britain by Cordee, 3a DeMontfort
Street, Leicester, England, LE1 7HD

First edition: first printing 1994, second printing 1995, third printing
1998, fourth printing 2001.

Manufactured in the United States of America

Edited by Miriam Bulmer
Maps by Tom Kirkendall
All photographs by Tom Kirkendall and Vicky Spring
Cover design by Watson Graphics
Book design by Marge Mueller
Typesetting and layout by The Mountaineers Books

Cover photograph: Hiker in Preston Park on Siyeh Pass Trail (trip 33)

Library of Congress Cataloging-in-Publication Data
Spring, Vicky, 1953-   .
    Glacier National Park and Waterton Lakes National Park : a
recreation guide / photos by Tom Kirkendall and Vicky Spring.
        p.   cm.
    Published simultaneously in Canada and Great Britain.
    Includes index.
    ISBN 0-89886-367-8
    1. Outdoor recreation--Montana--Glacier National Park--Guidebooks.
2. Outdoor recreation--Alberta--Waterton Lakes National Park--
Guidebooks. 3. Glacier National Park (Mont.)--Guidebooks. 4. Waterton
Lakes National Park (Alta.)--Guidebooks. I. Kirkendall, Tom. II. Title.
GV191.42.M9K57   1994
796.5'09786'52--dc20   93-48907
                                                               CIP

Distinctive fence near Belly River Ranger Station and snow-frosted Bear Mountain

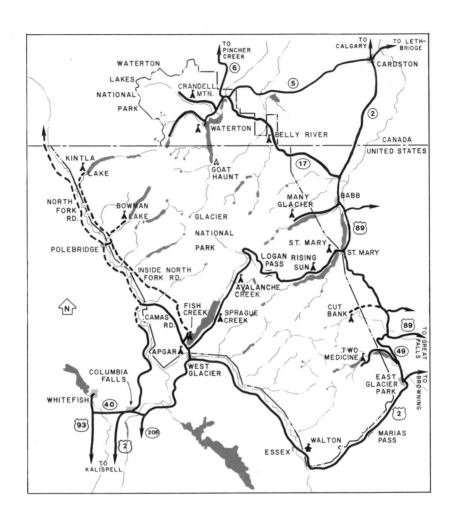

CONTENTS

INTRODUCTION   9

GLACIER NATIONAL PARK   33

LAKE McDONALD (West Glacier/Apgar/Lake McDonald) 35
Day Hikes and Backpacks
  1 Apgar Lookout 40
  2 Mount Brown Lookout and Snyder Lakes 42
  3 Sperry Chalet 44
  4 Sacred Dancing Cascade Loop 47
  5 Trout and Arrow Lakes 49
  6 Avalanche Lake 51
  7 Lake McDonald Trail 53
  8 Logging Lake Trail 55
Bicycling
  9 The Middle Fork Ride 57
  10 North Lake McDonald Road 59
  11 North Fork Loop 61
  12 Going-to-the-Sun Road 66
POLEBRIDGE   75
Day Hikes and Backpacks
  13 Bowman Lake.. 76
  14 Numa Ridge Lookout 78
  15 Quartz Lakes Loop 80
  16 Kintla Lake and the Boulder Pass Trail 82
Bicycling
  17 Bowman Lake.. 85
  18 Kintla Lake 87
WALTON   90
Day Hikes and Backpacks
  19 Scalplock Mountain Lookout 91
  20 Nyack–Coal Creek Wilderness Camping Zone 94
TWO MEDICINE AND EAST GLACIER PARK   97
Day Hikes and Backpacks
  21 Scenic Point 100
  22 Two Medicine Lake Circuit 102

23 Cobalt Lake 104
24 Upper Two Medicine Lake 107
25 Dawson Pass Loop 108
26 Firebrand Pass 111
CUT BANK   114
Day Hikes and Backpacks
27 Triple Divide Pass 115
Bicycling
28 Cut Bank 117
ST. MARY   120
Day Hikes and Backpacks
29 Red Eagle Lake 123
30 Otokomi Lake 125
31 The Falls Hike 127
32 Gunsight Lake 129
33 Siyeh Pass 131
Bicycling
34 St. Mary to Waterton Park 133
LOGAN PASS   139
Day Hikes and Backpacks
35 Hidden Lake 141
36 The Garden Wall 144
MANY GLACIER   146
Day Hikes and Backpacks
37 Cracker Lake 150
38 Grinnell Lake 152
39 Grinnell Glacier 153
40 Iceberg Lake 155
41 Ptarmigan Tunnel 158
42 Swiftcurrent Pass 160
43 The Northern Circle 162
44 Belly River 165
GOAT HAUNT   168
Day Hikes and Backpacks
45 Kootenai Lakes 171
46 Boulder Pass Trail—East Side 173

WATERTON LAKES NATIONAL PARK   175
Day Hikes and Backpacks
47 Bertha Lake and Falls 181

48 Waterton Lakeshore Trail 182
49 Crypt Lake 185
50 Goat Lake 187
51 Twin Lakes Loop 189
52 Lineham Falls 191
53 Rowe Lakes 193
54 Lineham Ridge and Lineham Lakes 195
55 Carthew–Alderson Traverse 197
56 Forum and Wall Lakes 199
Bicycling
57 Wishbone (Bosporus) Trail 201
58 Crandell Lake Loop 203
59 Bauerman Creek Valley (Snowshoe Trail) 207
60 Wall Lake 209

WINTER 211

WEST GLACIER   216
61 Going-to-the-Sun Road 217
62 McGee Meadow Loop 219
63 Fish Creek Campground 221
POLEBRIDGE   223
64 Big Prairie 224
65 Bowman Lake................................ 227
ESSEX—IZAAK WALTON INN   229
66 Ole Creek Trail 231
67 Marias Pass–Autumn Creek Trail 233
EAST GLACIER PARK   235
68 Two Medicine Lake 235
ST. MARY   238
69 Red Eagle Lake 239
70 St. Mary Lake................................. 241
71 Bullhead Lake 243
72 Grinnell Lake 245
WATERTON TOWNSITE   247
73 Cameron Lake Ski Trail 248
74 Wall Lake 250

Useful Addresses 252
Index 253

A Note About Safety

Safety is an important concern in all outdoor activities. No guidebook can alert you to every hazard or anticipate the limitations of every reader. Therefore, the descriptions of roads, trails, routes, and natural features in this book are not representations that a particular place or excursion will be safe for your party. When you follow any of the routes described in this book, you assume responsibility for your own safety. Under normal conditions, such excursions require the usual attention to traffic, road and trail conditions, weather, terrain, the capabilities of your party, and other factors. Keeping informed on current conditions and exercising common sense are the keys to a safe, enjoyable outing.

The Mountaineers

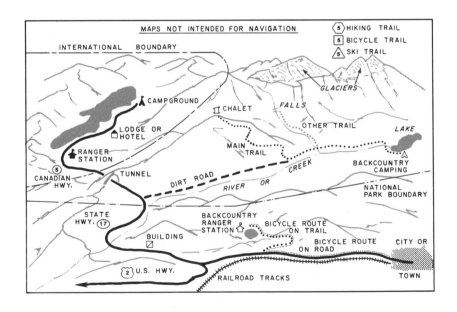

Opposite: *View of Lake Ellen Wilson with Gunsight Pass in distance*

INTRODUCTION

Waterton–Glacier International Peace Park

In 1932, Waterton Lakes National Park in Alberta and Glacier National Park in Montana were joined together in the world's first International Peace Park. The park was formed in honor of the co-operation and friendship between Canada and the United States, and in recognition that the rare and delicate ecosystem of the northern Rockies should not be bound by arbitrary political boundaries. Waterton–Glacier International Peace Park has set a standard for the rest of the world.

The formation of Waterton–Glacier International Peace Park was done in an astute manner that has encouraged the two parks to work together and, at the same time, retain their unique cultural identities. The International Peace Park is in reality two independent parks that share a common goal of preserving a single ecosystem from such encroachments of modern civilization as logging, mining, amusement parks, and overuse. The two parks collaborate in the important areas of wildlife management, resource protection, fire suppression, environmental education, visitor communication, and transportation.

However, the parks are two separate administrative entities.

Ptarmigan in summer plumage

Going-to-the-Sun Road at base of Clements Mountain near Logan Pass

Visitors must pay two separate entrance fees and follow two slightly different sets of rules. Visitors who cross the international boundary, in either direction, will notice enough cultural and philosophical differences between the two parks to enable them to savor the subtle thrill of visiting a foreign country.

Geology

The formation of the area we now know as Glacier and Waterton Lakes National Parks began sometime between 1,600 million and 800 million years ago. At that time the area was covered with a shallow sea. To the north, east, and south were highlands. Rivers carried sediments from the highlands to the sea, where, after millions of years of accumulation, rocks were formed. The beautiful colors of rocks found in both parks are the result of their watery origins. Ripple marks and fossilized algae that lived in the shallow sea bottoms can be seen in some formations.

Then, around 160 million years ago, a collision of the crustal plates occurred along the western edge of the North American continent. The pressures of this collision caused the land mass to buckle and fold, and a mountain chain rose out of the old sea bed to form the Rockies. It was an amazing, and slow, process that lasted almost 100 million years. Great hunks of the earth were folded, con-

Ripple preserved in sandstone

torted, and shattered. Huge masses of hard, old rock were shoved up and over much younger and softer rocks. The Lewis Overthrust, viewed from the Chief Mountain International Highway in Waterton Lakes, is an example of 600-million-year-old strata overlaying 100-million-year-old strata.

When the growth phase ended, around 60 million years ago, erosion became the major force in shaping this area. The tall mountains became rounded, and rivers cut broad valleys.

It was not until the Ice Age, just 2 million years ago, that this area underwent the transformation that sculpted it to the shape we are familiar with today. Huge rivers of ice filled the valleys and flowed down to the plains, carving the knife-edged ridges called *aretes* (the Garden Wall is an example), the horn-shaped mountains (such as Clements Mountain), and the deep U-shaped valleys (such as the upper McDonald Creek valley).

The Ice Age ended a mere 20,000 years ago, and the last of the huge valley glaciers disappeared from the Northern Rockies just 12,000 years ago. Since that time the world has seen numerous climatic fluctuations. During the early 1800s cool temperatures prevailed and once more the glaciers grew, surging off the sides of the mountains and heading down toward the valleys. Then, around the mid-1800s, the glaciers began a retreat that is still going on today. All glaciers in Glacier National Park have shrunk since the 1860s, and some have completely disappeared. No glaciers remain in Waterton Lakes National Park.

A Very Brief History

The hundreds of archaeological sites in Glacier and Waterton parks provide proof that Native peoples have used this area for at least 11,000 years. Plains Indians used the parks for hunting and religious purposes. Other Indians dwelt along the lakeshores for some or all of the year.

Today Indians are still an important part of the park. The eastern boundary of Glacier National Park borders on Blackfeet Nation lands, and along a portion of the eastern boundary of Waterton Lakes National Park are lands owned by the Blood Indians. The best places to learn more about the life and culture of the Indians are at the Head-Smashed-In Buffalo Jump, a World Heritage Site, located northeast of the town of Waterton Park, and at the excellent exhibits in the Museum of the Plains Indian in Browning, Montana.

The first white men to come into this area were fur trappers, traders, and missionaries, many of whom were associated with the Hudson's Bay Company. These early explorers were soon followed by miners, loggers, whiskey traders, and ranchers.

The Waterton Lakes area was first explored and chronicled by Thomas Blakiston in 1858. He is attributed with naming the lakes in honor of an English naturalist, Charles Waterton. Glacier National Park was given its name for commercial reasons by a Senator Carter, and many of the names of prominent park features were chosen to promote tourism rather than for historical reasons.

The Great Northern Railroad helped to popularize the parks, building large and stately hotels to house visitors. The railroad also sponsored a system of seven chalets around the parks, and visitors were taken from chalet to chalet on horseback. In 1933, the Going-to-the-Sun Road was opened and the era of the automobile tourist began. The chalet system lost popularity, and horses gave way to hikers.

Waterton Lakes Forest Reserve was created in 1895; Glacier National Park was created in 1910. The International Peace Park was a concept developed jointly by the Rotarians of Alberta and Montana. It was through their efforts that legislation was passed in 1932 in both the Canadian Parliament and the U.S. Congress that allowed formation of the Peace Park.

Waterton–Glacier International Peace Park became a Biosphere Preserve in the late 1970s, as part of a UNESCO program whose purpose is to protect examples of the world's ecosystem types to be used for scientific and research studies.

Getting to the Parks—Alternatives to Driving

If the long drive to Waterton–Glacier International Peace Park does not sound appealing, consider two other popular options: train or plane.

The train means Amtrak. There are two major stations: the Glacier Park Station, located on the east side of the park at the small town of East Glacier Park, Montana, and the West Glacier Station (formally known as the Belton Station), in the town of West Glacier, Montana, at the southwest corner of the park. There is also a small station in Essex, on the south side of Glacier National Park.

The closest major airports are located 130 miles (208 km) southeast of the parks, at Great Falls, Montana, and 200 miles (320 km) north of the parks, at Calgary, Alberta. Airports with commercial flights are located in Kalispell, Montana, 30 miles (50 km) southwest of West Glacier, and at Lethbridge, Alberta, 75 miles (121 km) northeast of Waterton.

Rental cars are available at all airports and train stations. From May 15 to September 25, trains at the Glacier Park and West Glacier stations are met by park concession buses.

Transportation in the Parks

The roads of Waterton Lakes and Glacier national parks are narrow, winding two-laners built for aesthetics rather than for rapid transit. In midsummer, when the traffic is heaviest, a drive through the park can be a slow, nerve-wracking experience.

The most difficult road to drive is the very popular and immeasurably beautiful Going-to-the-Sun Road. In order to reduce congestion on the Sun Road, as it is popularly known, the park plans restrictions on large vehicles, closing part of the road to vehicles and vehicle combinations more than 20 feet long and 7.5 feet wide (including mirrors). The restrictions apply only to the section of road from Avalanche Creek Campground on the west side of Logan Pass to Sun Point on the east side, a distance of 25 miles.

Bicycle use is also restricted on the Going-to-the-Sun Road. From June 15 through Labor Day, two sections of road are closed to

Red Bus tour at busy Logan Pass parking area

bicycling from 11:00 A.M. to 4:00 P.M. These are the 7.4-mile section of road around Lake McDonald from Apgar Campground to Sprague Creek Campground, and the 11.4-mile section of road along the Garden Wall from Logan Creek to Logan Pass.

Shuttles and buses offer viable alternatives to driving in Glacier and Waterton Lakes national parks. In Glacier, shuttle buses cruise the Going-to-the-Sun Road from the KOA Campground, outside the West Entrance, to St. Mary, on the east side of the park. Signs along the road note bus stops and times. The shuttles are especially convenient for hikers who want to spend part of the day hiking at Logan Pass or who would like to start their hike in one place and end it somewhere else.

The vintage Red Buses with the roll-back tops provide transportation from the train station to the hotels and from the hotels to all other hotels and major destination points in Glacier National Park. There is also a daily bus between the Glacier Park Lodge in East Glacier Park and the Prince of Wales Hotel in Waterton Lakes. The Red Buses offer one-way trips, round trips, and tours. For information and reservations, write, from mid-October to May, to Glacier Park, Inc., Dial Tower, Phoenix, AZ 85077-0928; from May to mid-October, call (406) 226-5551 (in the United States) or (403) 236-3400 (in Canada).

In Waterton Lakes National Park, a hikers' shuttle makes daily morning runs up the Akamina Parkway to Cameron Lake. Other destinations are available on request. Check at the Tamarack Mall in the Waterton townsite (officially called Waterton Park) for current schedules and fees.

Weather

When packing for a vacation in the Waterton–Glacier area, take a little time to think about the weather. On a typical day in July and August, temperatures are in the high 70s (mid-20s Celsius) in the valleys and the mid-50s (about 10 degrees Celsius) in the high country around Logan Pass. At night the temperatures are in the low 40s (about 5 degrees Celsius). Unfortunately, the weather is rarely "typical" in the mountains. Heat waves may settle in for weeks at a time during the summer, and temperatures can soar to the upper 90s (nearly 40 degrees Celsius). Snow is equally possible. In August 1992, the temperature was 97 degrees (36 degrees Cel-

Clouds boiling over Crandell Mountain, Waterton National Park

sius) at Apgar, Montana, on the 21st and a foot of snow covered the ground on the 23rd.

Come to the parks prepared for any kind of weather. Bring T-shirts and sunscreen for the warm days, but don't forget to pack a warm jacket, raincoat, hat, and mittens for the cold days.

When to Visit

Summer in the Rocky Mountains of northern Montana and southern Alberta is very short. The winter snowpack often lingers in the mountains until mid-July. Winterlike weather is not unusual in September. To be on the safe side, it is best to join the crowds and visit the parks in July and August.

Where to Stay

Campgrounds

For aesthetic and economic reasons, camping is the most popular form of lodging in the parks. During the months of July and August, the eleven campgrounds in Glacier National Park and the three campgrounds in Waterton Lakes National Park begin filling up by midmorning. There is no system for reservations, so visitors who arrive late must look to the private campgrounds at the outskirts of the parks.

Groups of eight to twenty-four people may stay in the group camps at Apgar, Many Glacier, St. Mary, and Two Medicine in Glacier National Park, and at Belly River Campground in Waterton Lakes National Park. Contact the Glacier or Waterton Lakes park headquarters for information (see The Useful Addresses section).

Park campgrounds provide running water, and most have flush toilets. Utility hookups are available only at Waterton Townsite Campground; however, the larger campgrounds have disposal stations. Campgrounds in Waterton Lakes have cooking shelters with tables and wood stoves; wood is provided. The smaller campgrounds—Belly River in Waterton Lakes, and Cut Bank, Kintla Lake, Bowman Lake, and Sprague Creek in Glacier—are set up to accommodate tents.

Campground opening dates are staggered from early May through mid-June. The campgrounds begin to close down right after the first weekend in September, although some are open to primitive camping until they are closed by snow. St. Mary Camp-

ground and the Apgar Picnic Area in Glacier and the Pass Creek Picnic Area in Waterton Lakes are open for primitive camping during the fall, winter, and spring.

Showers. After spending a week or so hiking around the park, most campers begin to search for a shower. In Glacier, showers are available at Rising Sun and Many Glacier and tokens can be purchased at the camp stores. The Waterton Townsite Campground has showers and hot water in the rest rooms. Showers are also available at most of the private camp areas around the perimeter of the parks.

Laundry Facilities. Laundromats are located at West Glacier, St. Mary, Many Glacier, and the Waterton townsite.

Hotels and Motels

Hotels and motels in Glacier National Park are run by Glacier Park, Inc. Reservations for the months of July and August should be made by mid-February. For information and reservations, from mid-October to May, write to Glacier Park, Inc., Dial Tower, Phoenix, AZ 85077-0928 or call (602) 207-6000; from May to mid-October, write to Glacier Park, Inc., East Glacier Park, MT 59434-0147 or call (406) 226-5551.

Alberta Tourism is extremely helpful in providing information about lodging in Waterton Lakes National Park. Their toll-free number is (800) 661-1222. Reservations should be made by mid-February for the following summer. If you plan to stay at the Prince of Wales Hotel, reservations must be made through Glacier Park, Inc.

Hostels

Hostels provide inexpensive accommodations for the budget traveler. The hostel in East Glacier Park is open from May 1 to October 15 and is within easy walking distance of the train station. For further information, write to Brownies Grocery and Hostel, Box 229, East Glacier Park, MT 59434, or call (406) 226-4426. The hostel in Polebridge has no easy access whatsoever. Because accommodations in Polebridge are extremely limited, it is best to make reservations ahead of time; write to the North Fork Hostel, Box 1, Polebridge, MT 59928, or phone (406) 888-5241.

Opposite: *Many Glacier Hotel, located on shore of Swiftcurrent Lake*

High Mountain Chalets

Located in high mountain meadows, the Sperry and Granite Park chalets rank among the most exotic lodgings in Glacier National Park. The chalets are in reality mountain hotels for hikers. They traditionally open July 1 and close Labor Day. If you are looking for cheap sleeps, the chalets are not the place. However, for comfortable lodging, excellent meals, and unforgettable locations, the chalets are unbeatable.

If hiking is not a favored mode of locomotion, horse trips to Granite Park Chalet and Sperry Chalet can be arranged through the Glacier Park Outfitters. Make reservations with the outfitters well ahead of time by writing to 8320 Hazel Avenue, Orangevale, CA 95662, from mid-September to mid-May, or to Many Glacier Stable, Box 295, Babb, MT 59411, the rest of the year.

In 1993, the Sperry and Granite Park chalets were closed for renovation until further notice. Because of the short summers in the mountains, the work is expected to take several years. The earliest possible reopening date for the chalets is the summer of 1996. At the time of this writing, it is uncertain whether Belton Chalet,

Garden Wall Trail to Granite Park Chalet

Sleeping quarters at Sperry Chalet

Inc., the chalets' operator for the last forty years, will continue to run the chalets when they reopen. Contact Glacier National Park for additional information and updates (see the Useful Addresses section).

Activities in the Parks

Day Hiking

This is the most popular activity in the parks. Day walks require only a bare minimum of planning. Bring a small day pack for the essentials, including food, lots of water, extra clothes, sunscreen, and sunglasses. You should also carry a map, such as the park handouts or a topographical map. Because there is always a chance of encountering bears on the trail, it is best to walk in a group and talk, shout occasionally, or sing as you go. You may also wear or carry some kind of noisemaking device such as a can of rocks, or a walking stick with bells. (Bear bells may be purchased at most park stores, but there is some debate about their effectiveness.)

Hiking season begins early in the parks. By May visitors begin exploring the lowland forest trails. However, it is not until mid-June to early July that the winter snowpack has melted sufficiently to allow hikers into the high alpine backcountry. If you plan to hike the high country during the late spring, it is advisable to carry an ice axe and know how to use it.

Backpacking

This is an activity that requires a great deal of planning before you leave home. Pack the Ten Essentials (map, compass, flashlight, food, clothing, sunglasses, first-aid supplies, pocket knife, water-proof matches, and fire starter), then add cooking gear, a tent (bears tend to respect a structure more than a person lying out unprotected), and a sleeping bag. Open fires are not allowed at many of the backcountry camps, so carry a stove for cooking and for boiling water. (Water in the backcountry should be boiled for five minutes before drinking to kill *Giardia* protozoa).

This is bear country. In Glacier, backpackers are required to carry a 25-foot piece of cord for hanging food out of the bears' reach. In Waterton Lakes, elevated platforms are provided, and cord is not necessary.

Backpackers are required to camp in designated backcountry camp areas, except in the Nyack–Coal Creek Wilderness Camping Zone in

Backpackers crossing Quartz Creek (trip 15)

Glacier and the Lineham Lakes Basin in Waterton Lakes. Camping in the designated areas is limited to the number of sites available; backcountry permits are required for all overnight camping.

In Glacier, backcountry use permits are issued at no charge from the following locations: Apgar Visitor Center, St. Mary Visitor Center, Two Medicine Ranger Station, and Many Glacier Ranger Station. The permits are given on a "first-come" basis and must be issued in person. They are available starting at 8:00 A.M. the day before the trip. In Waterton Lakes, backcountry use permits are issued free of charge on the day of the trip only. The permits may be obtained from the Information Centre located on the eastern edge of the townsite.

Early-season backpackers are often faced with large snow slopes at the passes. These snow slopes can be dangerous, and it is best to either hike around them or carry an ice axe for self-arrests in case of a fall. Trail bridges on the major rivers and streams are often not replaced until after the snowmelt, normally mid- to late-June. Most of these rivers are too dangerous to ford during the runoff season. Follow the advice of the ranger who issues the backcountry use permits and stick to the lowlands in the early summer.

Guide Services

Glacier Wilderness Guides offers day trips and backpack trips into the Glacier backcountry. Camping equipment may be rented. For information, write Box 535, West Glacier, MT 59936, or call (800) 521-RAFT.

Bicycling

In Glacier National Park bicycles are allowed only on established roadways and bike paths. Wheeled vehicles (bicycles) are not permitted on hiking or horse trails. Bicycle use is also restricted on the Going-to-the-Sun Road (see the Transportation in the Parks section).

For the touring cyclist, Glacier National Park has set aside a limited number of campsites at Apgar, Fish Creek, Sprague Creek, Avalanche Creek, Rising Sun, and St. Mary campgrounds. These campsites are reserved for bicyclists as well as pedestrians and motorcyclists. Each site has a metal storage box for food and supplies. Site capacity is eight people, and a fee is charged per person.

Waterton Lakes National Park has four specific trails open to mountain bikes. Cyclists are also welcome on all paved roads.

Riding a bicycle in bear country has its own special challenges. Bicycles move rapidly along forest roads and trails, and the chances of surprising a bear are much greater than for slower-moving hikers. Remember to make as much noise as possible when rounding corners in the woods; yell, talk loudly, sing, or ring an obnoxiously loud bike bell. Stay away from areas where bears have been sighted.

Fishing

No license is required to fish in Glacier National Park, making it a popular activity with many visitors. The park produces a pamphlet detailing all fishing regulations. You can pick up a copy at any ranger station or visitor center.

Glacier National Park ended the practice of stocking lakes when it was determined that the native fish populations were suffering. Therefore, fishing can be a challenging business. In the larger lakes, the fish are easiest to catch where the water is deepest, and boats or rafts are very helpful. Fishermen without watercraft are advised to hike to some of the smaller mountain lakes. For details and helpful hints, pick up a copy of *Fishing Glacier National Park* by Paul Hintzen, published by the Glacier Natural History Association.

Fishing conditions in Waterton Lakes National Park are similar to those in Glacier. The only major difference is that a license is required. These may be purchased at the Information Centre in the Waterton townsite.

Boating and Water Sports

Bring your own watercraft or rent one in either Waterton Lakes or Glacier National Park. Boat launch ramps are available at McDonald, Bowman, Two Medicine, St. Mary, and Middle and Upper Waterton lakes. Boat rentals (canoes, rowboats, and motorboats) are available at McDonald, Two Medicine, Swiftcurrent, and Cameron lakes.

Waterskiing is permitted on McDonald, St. Mary, and Middle and Upper Waterton lakes. Windsurfing is allowed on all lakes. Motorboats on Bowman and Two Medicine lakes are limited to 10 hp or less. No motors are allowed on Kintla Lake.

Canoes and kayaks are popular for exploring the wilderness lakes. Bowman, Kintla, McDonald, and Waterton lakes have backcountry campsites where canoes and kayaks may be beached.

Rental boats at Cameron Lake

Overnight stays at these sites require a backcountry use permit. Canoe carts are not permitted on backcountry trails.

All the large lakes in Glacier and Waterton Lakes are subject to sudden high winds. Small boats such as canoes and kayaks should be used with caution. Stay close to shore and beach your boat when the wind-driven waves become too high for safe paddling.

White-water canoeing, kayaking, and rafting are common on the Middle and North Fork Flathead rivers in Montana and on the Belly River in Alberta. Information about white-water activities is available through both parks' headquarters. However, if you need to know about current conditions on the Flathead River, contact the Flathead National Forest office in Kalispell (see The Useful Addresses section).

Horseback Riding

Saddle horse rides are offered from Apgar Corral, Lake McDonald Corral, and Many Glacier Corral in Glacier, and Alpine Stables in Waterton Lakes. Ride lengths vary from one hour to all day. Alpine Stables also offers pack trips, by reservation only.

For details on riding in Glacier, contact Glacier Park Outfitters,

Guided horseback trip at Granite Park

Inc. at 8320 Hazel Avenue, Orangevale, CA 95662, from mid-September through mid-May, and at Many Glacier Stable, Box 295, Babb, MT 59411, during the rest of the year. For more information about the Alpine Stables in Waterton Lakes, write to P.O. Box 53, Waterton Park, AB T0K 2M0.

Wild Animals

Bears

The first thing many people think of when Glacier and Waterton Lakes national parks are mentioned is ferocious grizzly bears. The media have expounded and expanded on the testy temperament of the park grizzly bears, and sensationalized each incident to the point that the bears have gained a reputation for bloodthirsty and unpredictable behavior unequaled on this continent.

The reputation of the grizzlies has enchanted our love of the sensational and scared us silly at the same time. Many park visitors feel cheated if they do not see a grizzly in the park and, at the same time, are so frightened of the bears that they are afraid to get out of their cars except at the visitor centers.

If the idea of hiking, bicycling, or camping with bears is worrisome, take a look at some very reassuring statistics. In 1992 there were an estimated 800 grizzly bears in the lower forty-eight states. Of these, 200 live within the boundaries of Glacier National Park. There are also 500 black bears in the park, which, from a distance, may be confused with grizzlies.

Signs are posted at trailheads after grizzly bears have been sighted.

Grizzly bear foraging in meadow near Swiftcurrent Lake

In an average year, Glacier National Park receives more than 2,000,000 visitors. During that same average year, there are approximately 2,500 bear sightings. In the last seven years, there have been an average of two maulings and 0.42 deaths a year. That means that, statistically, 1 out of 1,000,000 visitors may be mauled and 1 out every 4,761,905 visitors may be killed. Obviously you have a much greater chance of being killed in a traffic accident driving to and from the parks than by a bear.

When you enter the park, you will be given information concerning bears, with some sensible rules to help people and bears coexist. These are good rules, which require you to leave a clean campsite, stay away from the bears and all other wild animals, and, most important of all, don't feed the wild animals.

If you follow these rules, you have a good chance of enjoying a safe vacation. If you ignore these rules, you or someone who comes along after you may have serious trouble. You might even be the cause of a bear having to be destroyed.

Bears are extremely intelligent. They not only remember food found once in a campground or picninc area, they pass this information along to their offspring. To protect the bears, park officials diligently patrol the park looking for anyone who leaves coolers, food, or cooking paraphernalia where bears can find it. Remember, humans have it easy—we get citations and fines. If bears make a mistake, they get transported or shot.

Backpackers receive a lecture on bears every time they obtain a backcountry use permit. Again, these are very sensible rules. If you follow them, your chances of encountering a bear are minimal. Bears do not like to be surprised, so the number-one rule is to make noise while walking on the trail. Besides talking, singing, and loudly clapping hands whenever you are walking near a stream, going around a corner, or passing through dense vegetation, carry some kind of constant noisemaker to take up the slack when the vocal cords need a rest. Bear bells, one of the least effective noisemakers, may be purchased at numerous locations around the parks. If you choose to use bells, buy several and attach them to your pack, body, or shoes—as far away from your ears as possible. A pop can with a couple of rocks inside makes an equally repelling noise, if you remember to shake it. Be creative: bicycle horns, whistles, castanets, or anything that makes fairly continuous noise works well to warn bears that a human is on the trail. The best method for avoiding bear attacks is for hikers and backpackers to travel in large, noisy groups. Several people singing off-key or arguing politics is more than a normal bear can stand.

Of course, there are the people who value the peace and quiet of the wilderness more than they value their own lives or the lives of the bears. Before you join their ranks and take your chances, remember that most attacks on humans come from bears who were surprised and did not have time to move away before a hiker arrived.

There is a product on the market that is designed to protect you if you are attacked by a bear. This cayenne pepper spray has proven quite effective. However, both Glacier and Waterton Lakes are known for their windy weather, and you do not want to be downwind from a blast of pepper spray. So carry this product if it makes you feel more comfortable on the trail, but do not place total reliance on it. The spray can be purchased in Glacier National Park at the camp stores. (Note: as of this writing, it is illegal to transport the spray from the United States into Canada.)

The backcountry campsites are set up so that cooking and sleeping areas are separated. If you plan to do any hiking in Glacier National Park, be sure and pack 25 feet of lightweight cord and a

Hanging food and other gear at backcountry campsite

couple of sturdy stuff bags for hanging extra food, the clothes you cooked in, and any smelly toiletries, such as your toothbrush and toothpaste, sunscreen, and mosquito repellent.

There has been a lot of talk and speculation as to whether it is safe for women to hike when they are menstruating and whether sexual activity can attract bears. To date there is no conclusive proof showing that either of these two situations attracts bears. However, it never hurts to err on the side of caution.

One suggestion is to plan nonaromatic meals in the backcountry. Bears can smell cooking sausage and bacon for miles. Bland meals of rice, potatoes, or noodles have little or no odor and will sustain life without creating the enticing smells that attract bears.

If you see a bear while hiking, report the sighting to the ranger. If several sightings are made in the same area, the trail will be posted, warning other hikers of a possible bear encounter. If a bear acts aggressive, a ranger will be sent out to investigate. If the situation is potentially serious, such as a sow with cubs, the trail may be closed to hikers until the bears move on.

If you should encounter a bear on the trail, follow the rules listed in the park information handouts. Read the suggestions carefully, then think out your own plan of action ahead of time. Talk it over with your hiking partners so everyone is ready.

Mountain Lions

While most issues of visitors versus wildlife are focused on aggressive grizzly bears, there is a growing problem with mountain lions. The mountain lions, also known as cougars or pumas, were largely driven out or killed by the early settlers. Now these animals seem to be making a comeback.

Mountain lions are clever hunters and rarely seen by park visitors. Occasionally their tracks are spotted, but even that is unusual. In the last couple of years, however, there have been several attacks on young children. The best defense against potential cougar attacks is to keep the group together when hiking. Do not allow the kids to run ahead, out of sight of an adult. Do not allow one or several children to hike alone.

If someone in your party is attacked by a mountain lion, you must act aggressively; beat it with a stick and make loud noises. Do not act meek or attempt to play dead. Do not run for help. Act quickly, decisively, and with force.

The Trips and the Ratings

The hikes and backpacks described in here are designed for the "average" person. This somewhat mythical being moves along the trail at a steady 2-mile-an-hour pace with a 5-minute rest break every hour or so, a bit slower if the trail is very steep.

Real-life hikers are not robots. Paces will vary with the amount of elevation gain and the strength of the group. Use the information provided at the beginning of each trip to make your own itinerary for the hike.

Hikes and backpacks have not been rated for difficulty. Use the elevation gain listing at the beginning of each trip to determine whether or not the hike is appropriate for you. Except for trip 20, all trails described in this book are in excellent condition.

Bicycle Ratings

Bicycle trips are rated as easy, moderate, or difficult.

Easy. This category includes paved and well-maintained gravel roads with little elevation gain. No previous biking experience is necessary to enjoy these rides.

Moderate. Rides with this rating are often long and may have steep climbs. Road surfaces may be poorly maintained. These trips require considerable energy and some experience.

Difficult. This category is a catch-all for rides that do not fit the easy or moderate rating. Expect steep climbs, deep ruts, and narrow roads or trails. These trips are most enjoyable for cyclists with a lot of riding experience.

Further Information

For further information concerning park activities, contact the parks' headquarters. For Glacier, write to the Superintendent, Glacier National Park, West Glacier, MT 59936, or call (406) 888-5441. For Waterton Lakes, contact the Park Superintendent, Waterton Lakes National Park, AB T0K 2M0, or call (403) 859-2224.

For TDD service, call (406) 888-5790.

Opposite: *Lake McDonald*

GLACIER NATIONAL PARK

Avalanche Gorge (trip 6)

LAKE McDONALD
(West Glacier/Apgar/Lake McDonald)

The largest of the 250 lakes in Glacier National Park is 11-mile-long Lake McDonald. It lies in a broad, glacier-carved valley surrounded by tree-covered hillsides that come to an abrupt end at a towering barrier of mountains known as the Garden Wall.

Lake McDonald serves as a staging area for visits to the park. The nearby West Entrance Station is the one closest to airports and cities, and for many visitors this area offers their first glimpse of the park they have traveled so far to see. Weather is mild around the lake, making it a great base for further explorations and a delightful place to return to after spending a day in the wind on the east side of the park.

The Lake McDonald area has three separate "hubs." The first is the town of West Glacier, located just outside the park boundary at the Highway 2 turnoff. Two miles east, inside the park, is Apgar Village, situated on the shores of the lake. The third hub is the Lake McDonald Lodge complex, located near the upper end of the lake, 9 miles east of Apgar.

Accommodations And Services

In the Lake McDonald area, lodging is available both inside and outside the park. The most notable of the accommodations is regal Lake McDonald Lodge, which is actually a combination of a beautiful, stately old wooden hotel, a motel, and cabins. At Apgar Village there are two motels: the Village Inn Motel and the Apgar Village Lodge. There are also two motels in West Glacier and more lodging along Highway 2, west of the park. The largest concentration of motels outside of the park is in Kalispell and the neighboring ski resort town of Whitefish, 30 miles from West Glacier.

Campers have the choice of four areas around Lake McDonald. The Apgar Campground, near Apgar Village, has 196 sites, and nearby Fish Creek Campground has another 180 sites. Sprague Creek Campground, located near Lake McDonald Lodge, is a small,

25-site area that caters to tents. The 87-site Avalanche Campground is located about 4 miles above the upper end of Lake McDonald, at the edge of a grove of large cedars and at the start of a popular trail to Avalanche Lake (see trip 6).

Most campgrounds fill up by midmorning during the summer. For late arrivers, there are several private campgrounds located just west of the park entrance on Highway 2.

Evening programs, with a park naturalist, are held nightly at Lake McDonald Lodge, Apgar Amphitheater, Avalanche Campground, and the Fish Creek Campground. These programs may include a slide show or a movie and a question-and-answer period. Program schedules are posted in the campgrounds, at the Apgar Visitor Center, and at the lodge.

The town of West Glacier has three restaurants. Two miles away, at Apgar Village, there is a restaurant and a deli. At Lake McDonald Lodge, a formal dining room, a coffee shop, and a lounge serve guests and drop-ins.

Groceries, fishing gear, and camping supplies are available in West Glacier. The small camp stores at Apgar and Lake McDonald Lodge offer only the most basic of food supplies. T-shirts and souvenirs are available everywhere, with the largest concentration of gift shops being at Apgar.

West Glacier also has a laundromat, a post office, a camera shop, a one-hour photo lab, an eighteen-hole golf course, and two gas stations.

Activities

The best way to start your visit to the Lake McDonald area is with a trip to the Apgar Visitor Center. It is a small facility where you may talk with a ranger, buy maps and books, and inquire about current trail and weather conditions.

Guided Walks. One of the best ways to learn about the park is to take a naturalist-guided hike. Every day during the summer season you have three guided walks to choose from in the Lake McDonald area. From the Apgar Visitor Center, a naturalist leads a walk through the forest environment of lower McDonald Creek. At the upper end of Lake McDonald, there is a scenic and interesting walk through the woods to Johns Lake, then on to the Sacred Dancing Cascade. The most fascinating walk is the hike through Avalanche Gorge to beautiful Avalanche Lake (see trip 6).

Trail of the Cedars

Driving. The most popular activity for visitors in the Lake McDonald area is driving the Going-to-the-Sun Road to Logan Pass or St. Mary. When coupled with a hike at Logan Pass and numerous stops at the wayside exhibits, this is an all-day trip. However, it is not necessary to make this drive in a car. If the designated driver would like to relax and enjoy the spectacular scenery, take a bus. The vintage Red Buses, with the roll-back tops, depart from Lake McDonald Lodge and make full-day tours over Logan Pass to St. Mary and back. The shuttle buses make hourly runs from West Glacier to St. Mary and may be boarded or left at any of the designated stops along the Going-to-the-Sun Road.

Boating. Scenic boat cruises on Lake McDonald depart from the Lake McDonald Lodge dock and cruise the remote western shore of the lake. No stops are made on this 60-minute trip.

Private boats are allowed on the lake and may be launched from Apgar. Hand-carried boats and windsurfers may be launched anywhere along the lakeshore. If you didn't bring your own boat, rental rowboats, canoes, and 6-hp motorboats are available at Apgar and Lake McDonald Lodge.

Rafting. An exciting activity that the whole family will enjoy is a raft trip. Four rafting companies in West Glacier offer trips down the Middle Fork and the North Fork Flathead River, ranging from half days to whole days to several days. Rates and trips offered by the four companies are nearly identical.

Horseback Riding. There are two stables in the Lake McDonald area. The Apgar Corral is located near the West Entrance, and the Lake McDonald Corral is situated on the Going-to-the-Sun Road across from Lake McDonald Lodge. Both corrals offer rides that vary in length from one hour to all day. These rides are very popular, so phone ahead for reservations. To reach the Apgar

Bear tracks

Guided raft trip on Middle Fork Flathead River

Corral, call (406) 888-5522. To reach the Lake McDonald Corral, call (406) 888-5670.

Bicycling. Bicycles, the single-speed cruiser type, may be rented at the Apgar Village Inn. Bicycle riders are welcome to cruise the campground loops or follow the bike path from Apgar to the park headquarters, a 4-mile round trip. Unfortunately, the bike path crosses two very busy roads, and young children should be accompanied by an adult.

Short Hikes

Trail of the Cedars. This is a 0.8-mile loop trip, through a grove of 500- to 700-year-old western red cedars. The trail passes through a garden of ferns and near weeping rocks. Due to the dampness of the area, nearly half the path is on a boardwalk, making the loop suitable for wheelchairs. The trail begins 15.8 miles east of the West Glacier Entrance on the Going-to-the-Sun Road, just beyond Avalanche Creek Campground.

Huckleberry Mountain Nature Loop. This is a short and rugged 0.6-mile loop through an old burn area. The loop offers the opportunity to see a forest in the process of regeneration and to compare it with an old-growth area. The trail begins 300 feet west of the Camas Entrance Station, 12 miles north of Apgar Village.

Rocky Point. A 2-mile round trip on a level trail leads to a viewpoint on the shores of Lake McDonald. The hike begins in the Fish Creek Campground or from the Inside North Fork Road and is an ideal morning or afternoon stroll for anyone staying there.

Howe Lake. This 4-mile round trip gains only 240 feet on its way to a marshy lake in the forest. Moose are occasionally seen along the trail and at the lake. The hike begins 5.4 miles north of the Fish Creek Campground on the primitive Inside North Fork Road.

Day Hikes And Backpacks

1 Apgar Lookout

Round trip: 5.6 miles (9 km)
Elevation gain: 1856 feet (566 m)
High point: 5236 feet (1596 m)
Hiking time: 3 hours
Day hike

From the quiet wilderness of the Apgar Mountains, gaze out over the modern world, where high-tech rafters drift along the river,

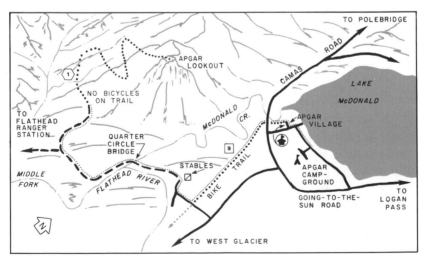

Middle Fork Flathead River valley viewed from Apgar Lookout

golfers buzz around immaculate greens in little white carts, trains ease out of a long series of tunnels and speed across the open valley, and a seemingly endless stream of motor vehicles zip in and out of the park.

This fascinating view is reached by a short, rather steep trail that climbs from the Middle Fork Flathead River valley to a fire lookout on the shoulder of the Apgar Mountains. Carry plenty of water, as none is available at the lookout, and wear sturdy shoes—the trail is coated with a layer of horse by-product.

Access: Drive from the West Entrance Station into the park for 0.3 mile, then turn left, following signs for "TRAIL RIDES." The paved road ends at the stables. Continue straight ahead on a dirt road for 0.5 mile to McDonald Creek and the Quarter Circle Bridge. If your vehicle is not designed to tackle rocks and deep potholes, or if you would simply like to extend the hike, park just before the bridge. The road continues on, paralleling the Middle Fork Flathead River. At the end of a mile the road divides. Go right for the final 0.5 mile to the parking area (elevation 3380 feet).

The Hike: Walk around the gate, then climb through forest following an old road for the first 0.8 mile. Once the trail leaves the road, it begins a steady climb toward the lookout. The views appear after the second switchback and continue to improve all the way to the summit.

The trail crests a ridge at 2.7 miles, then tunnels through high brush across a narrow saddle. A short, final climb leads to the lookout. Visitors are allowed to climb the lookout and wander around the balcony in search of views. If you carried a map, it's time to unfold it and identify the incredible panorama of summits extending from the park to the Flathead National Forest.

2 Mount Brown Lookout and Snyder Lakes

Round trip to Mount Brown Lookout: 10.6 miles (17 km)
Elevation gain: 4300 feet (1311 m)
High point: 7478 feet (2279 m)
Hiking time: 7 hours
Day hike

Round trip to lower Snyder Lake: 8.6 miles (13.8 km)
Elevation gain: 2035 feet (620 m)
High point: 5210 feet (1588 m)
Hiking time: 5 hours
Day hike or backpack

These are two excellent destinations, one leading to outstanding views, the other to an inviting subalpine lake.

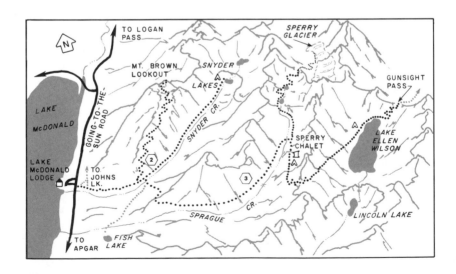

Mount Brown Lookout

Access: Drive the Going-to-the Sun Road for 11.2 miles east from its intersection with Highway 2 at West Glacier. Park at Lake McDonald Lodge (elevation 3175 feet).

The Hike: Both hikes begin by walking across the Going-to-the-Sun Road and following the Gunsight Pass–Sperry Chalet Trail through the forest. There are two junctions in the first 100 feet; stay right at both. The trail climbs, gaining nearly 1000 feet while paralleling the deep Snyder Creek Gorge for 1.6 miles to the Mount Brown Lookout Trail intersection.

The trail to the lookout is steep, climbing to the top in twenty-nine excruciating switchbacks. (The first five switchbacks are the steepest; if you survive them, you can make it all the way.) The lookout trail breaks out into meadows created by an old burn at switchback 24. Switchback 25 provides the first good view of the lookout, and the final switchback takes you to a high ridge top that is followed to the lookout and views.

The actual summit of 8565-foot-high Mount Brown appears just a long hop, skip, and jump to the northeast. Beyond Mount Brown, the Little Matterhorn and a small corner of the Sperry Glacier can be seen. Hills and summits and even mountain ranges extend out in all directions. To the west Lake McDonald is visible, stretching out to the base of the Apgar Mountains.

Hikers heading for Snyder Lakes will find their intersection just a few feet beyond the lookout trail. This popular trail climbs gradually, gaining only 1000 feet in the 2.7 miles to the backcountry campsite and the lower lake.

No formal trail exists between the lower and upper Snyder Lakes. The rough passage between the two lakes requires scrambling over rocks and through brush, around the right side of the lower lake, then up the hillside. The upper lake is the larger of the two and the more picturesque.

3 Sperry Chalet

Round trip: 13.6 miles (21.8 km)
Elevation gain: 3240 feet (988 m)
High point: 6440 feet (1963 m)
Hiking time: 2–3 days
Backpack

Sperry Chalet, the magnet that draws hikers to the beautiful subalpine Glacier Basin at the head of Sprague Creek, was closed for renovation in 1993. The earliest possible reopening date is the

Cook house and dining room at Sperry Chalet

summer of 1996. Check with the Park Service for updates. The nearby backcountry campground will be open throughout the chalet renovation.

Picturesque as the chalet, campground, and surrounding meadows seem, Glacier Basin is by no means the scenic highlight of the area. The chalet and neighboring backcountry campsite are simply a convenient, and scenic, base camp for hikes to the outstanding alpine country above.

Reservations for the chalet (when it is open) and nearby campground are hard to get. If you wish to stay at the chalet, make your reservations in January (see High Mountain Chalets in the Introduction). Camping permits are also at a premium. Plan to be at the visitor center by 8:00 A.M. the day before you intend to start your hike in order to reserve your site.

Access: From the West Entrance Station, drive east on the Going-to-the-Sun Road for 10.2 miles. Park at Lake McDonald Lodge (elevation 3200 feet). The hike begins directly across the road from the parking area. **(See map on page 44.)**

The Hike: Head into the forest, following the Gunsight Pass Trail. There are two junctions in the first 100 feet; stay to the right at both. The trail heads up the forested hillside, gaining nearly 1000 feet in the first 1.6 miles. The climb slackens and the trail passes the Mount Brown Lookout Trail intersection (see trip 2). A few feet beyond, the Snyder Lakes Trail branches off to the left. The trail dips to cross Snyder Creek at Crystal Ford (crossed on a wide bridge), where there is an intersection with the Fish Lake Trail.

At 2.5 miles the trail levels and the next mile is spent traversing a forested hillside, heading for the base of the next climb. This second climb is longer and steeper than the first and considerably more interesting. After the first couple of switchbacks the monotony is broken by a view of Beaver Medicine Falls. Shortly after, the trail enters a meadow and the views begin to expand. Before long, the chalet comes into view, perched on a rocky knoll, providing a tangible goal to those whose energies are flagging.

At 6.5 miles the trail to Sperry Glacier branches off on the left. Continue straight ahead, climbing the final 0.3 mile, to reach the chalet at 6.8 miles. Backpackers continue on with a gradual climb over the meadows for another 0.3 mile to the backcountry campsite.

Once you have set up camp, rested your legs, and cooled off your feet, it's time to head out to the high country.

Giant cairn marks trail to Sperry Glacier

Sperry Glacier: It's a 6.8-mile round-trip hike from the camp area to the glacier, with an elevation gain of 1600 feet. The well-graded trail traverses open meadows, passes waterfalls, and wanders near three small tarns on its way to the high country. Just below 8000-foot Comeau Pass lies a band of cliffs; the final push to the top is through a narrow cut in the rock. Steps have been created to aid the feet while a fixed rope aids the hands and the mind. The trail disappears at the pass and the route continues on over the stony ground, marked by a series of giant cairns. Remember: Do not walk on the glacier—crevasses may be hidden under the snow and help is a long way away for those who fall in.

Gunsight Pass: The pass is an 8.8-mile round-trip hike from the camp area, and although the total elevation gain is only 500 feet, the trail manages to climb more than 1500 feet. The entire hike is above timberline, and the views of the surrounding mountains, glaciers, meadows, and lakes make this one of the most exciting hikes in the park.

The trail leaves the camp area and climbs through meadows to a 7050-foot pass on the shoulder of Lincoln Peak, then descends to an open basin with views of Lincoln Lake and Beaver Chief Falls in an isolated valley below. After climbing a rocky rib, the trail begins a long descent along the length of Lake Ellen Wilson. It's a beautiful valley, but the descent is heartbreaking. After passing beneath a band of cliffs at the upper end of the lake, the trail reaches its 6000-foot low point and the climb to 6946-foot Gunsight Pass begins in earnest. The pass is worth the effort, with an outstanding view as your reward.

4 Sacred Dancing Cascade Loop

Loop trip: 5 miles (8 km)
Elevation gain: 200 feet (61 m)
High point: 3300 feet (1006 m)
Hiking time: 3 hours
Day hike

When inclement weather keeps you out of the high country, stretch the kinks out of your legs on this scenic forest ramble to Johns Lake, Sacred Dancing Cascade, and McDonald Falls.

Access: From the West Entrance Station, drive the Going-to-the-Sun Road east for 10.2 miles to Lake McDonald Lodge (elevation 3200 feet).

The Hike: To begin the loop, walk across the Going-to-the-Sun Road and hike up the Gunsight Pass Trail for 200 feet. Pass a spur trail to the stables and, when the trail divides a second time, go left and head up the forested valley on the Avalanche Trail. In spring and early summer the valley floor is dappled with delicate flowers;

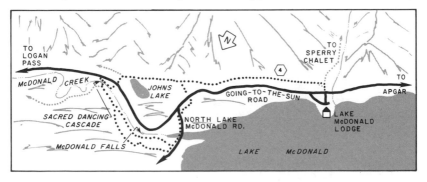

McDonald Falls

by midsummer it is awash with green from the bracken ferns, devil's club, and moss.

The trail divides several times; stay on the Avalanche Trail at all junctions. After 2 miles of walking, pass Johns Lake, a shallow pond where lilies and reeds grow in profusion. Just beyond, the trail divides again. Leave the Avalanche Trail here and take the left fork, which descends to Going-to-the-Sun Road.

Carefully cross the road, then walk up to a large turnout where a wide trail descends to McDonald Creek and the Sacred Dancing Cascade. On warm days this a popular area for picnics. On wet days, the center of the horse bridge has the best view of the cascade.

Once across the bridge, go left, heading back down the valley along the edge of McDonald Creek for 500 feet to an intersection. There are no trail signs here, so look for the "NO HORSES ALLOWED" sign and take the left fork. This foot trail parallels McDonald Creek for the next mile, passing McDonald Falls before ending at North Lake McDonald Road. Go left, crossing McDonald Creek on the car bridge, then walk to the opposite side of the road and follow the trail along the edge of the pavement for 500 feet before heading through the trees to Going-to-the-Sun Road.

Carefully recross the road, then follow the trail up the forested hillside for 500 feet to rejoin the Avalanche Trail for the final 1.5 miles back to Lake McDonald Lodge.

5 Trout and Arrow Lakes

Round trip to Trout Lake: 7 miles (11.2 km)
Elevation gain: 2000 feet in (610 m); 1300 feet out (396 m)
High point: 4200 feet (1280 m)
Hiking time: 5 hours
Day hike

Round trip to Arrow Lake: 13.2 miles (21.1 km)
Elevation gain: 2100 feet in (640 m); 1300 feet out (396 m)
High point: 4200 feet (1280 m)
Hiking time: 2 days
Backpack

Although it is just a 3.5-mile hike into the spectacular Camas Creek valley, this quiet wilderness area with its meadows, six lakes, views, and excellent fly fishing is overlooked by most park visitors. There is a twofold reason for this. First, the trailhead is accessed via a narrow dirt road that is rough and full of deep potholes. Second, this is prime grizzly bear habitat.

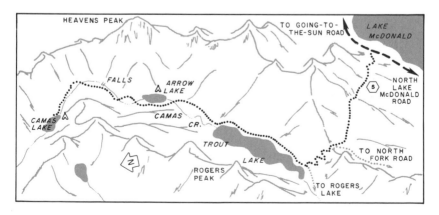

Trout Lake

The Lake McDonald Lodge stables offers all-day trail rides to Trout and Arrow lakes, an alternative for those who don't like the idea of hiking a trail that is shared with bears.

Access: From the West Entrance Station, drive the Going-to-the-Sun Road east 11.7 miles to the upper end of Lake McDonald. Turn left on the North Lake McDonald Road (unsigned) and follow it for 2 miles to a small parking area and trailhead (elevation 3230 feet).

The Hike: The first 2.5 miles are spent climbing steeply up a forested hillside to the 4200-foot crest of Howe Ridge. Just before the top, the Howe Ridge Fire Trail branches off to the left. (This rarely used trail follows the forested ridge crest west. It is well marked but generally very brushy.) Continue straight, across a forested saddle, then descend 1300 feet to the floor of the Camas Creek valley.

At 3.2 miles, the narrow, wet, and brushy trail to Rogers Lake and the lower Camas Creek valley branches off on the left. Passing the intersection, continue on for another 0.3 mile to Trout Lake. For day hikers the small beach alongside the trail is an ideal picnic spot and turnaround point.

Backpackers must continue on to Arrow Lake to find the backcountry campsites. The trail heads up the south side of Trout

Lake, crossing avalanche slopes with stunning views of Rogers and Heavens peaks.

At 7 miles the trail reaches Arrow Lake and the backcountry campsite. Hikers who plan to spend several nights in the valley might like to visit Camas Lake, a scenic, though somewhat brushy, 7-mile round-trip day hike from Arrow Lake. It is also possible to spend the night at Camas Lake in the backcountry campground.

6 Avalanche Lake

Round trip: 4 miles (6 km)
Elevation gain: 560 feet (171 m)
High point: 3905 feet (1190 m)
Hiking time: 3 hours
Day hike

Originating in the frozen mass of ice called the Sperry Glacier, rivulets of melting water come together to form creeks. These creeks descend the broad, sloping Sperry Glacier plateau, then plunge 2000 feet down perpendicular cliffs to rest, temporarily, in the emerald waters of Avalanche Lake. Slowly the water meanders down the lake, picking up speed as it is siphoned into Avalanche Creek. The speed increases, and in a couple of miles the waters are once again crashing and churning. The sheer force and unchained power of this stream has cut Avalanche Gorge, a deep channel through the bedrock where the water swirls and churns its way down a series of cascades. Beyond the gorge, water flows through a

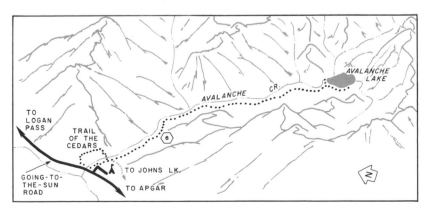

Ranger-led hike at Avalanche Lake

stately grove of western red cedars before joining McDonald Creek for a roller-coaster ride to McDonald Lake.

The journey of Avalanche Creek is a sight worth seeing, and during the summer hundreds of hikers make the easy trek along the creek to the shores of Avalanche Lake every day.

Access: From the West Entrance Station, drive the Going-to-the-Sun Road east for 15.7 miles to the Avalanche Campground. Turn into the campground and park near the entrance at the trailhead. If that parking area is full, try parking at the picnic area just across the road.

The Hike: Begin your hike with a stroll through a grove of western red cedars on the Trail of the Cedars nature loop. Pass a rest room and a water fountain before the trail divides. Go right, heading uphill to a second intersection, where you take the left fork. The trail climbs above Avalanche Gorge, then eases into a forest ramble for 2 shady miles to the lake.

You can stop as soon as you reach the lakeshore and eat your lunch on a small bench, or you can continue on to the upper end of the lake by walking the trail or the gravel beach along the lakeshore. After 0.5 mile, you are rewarded with a view of the lower portion of Monument Falls, where the foaming waters cover the rock wall in a sheet of white. The trail ends abruptly at the head of the lake. Beyond is a wall of brush, best left for the deer, bear, and other citizens of the park.

7 Lake McDonald Trail

Round trip to Lake McDonald Campsite: 9.2 miles (14.8 km)
Elevation gain: 150 feet (46 m)
High point: 3200 feet (975 m)
Hiking time: 5 hours
Day hike or backpack

This forested trail traverses the west shore of Lake McDonald from Fish Creek Campground to the North Lake McDonald Road. It is ideally located for guests at Fish Creek Campground who may want to stretch the kinks out of their legs after a long day of driving. It is also the perfect trail for days when the dense forest around the lakeshore is preferable to the dripping clouds and chill winds that frequently chase hikers out of the high country.

If transportation can be arranged, the trail may be hiked as a 7-mile one-way trip between the two trailheads. However, for most people, a round trip to the obvious turnaround points—Rocky Point at 0.8 mile, the lakeshore at 1.8 miles, or the backcountry campground at 4.6 miles—is preferable to the rather complicated business of arranging transportation at each end of the trail.

Access: Campers can find the trail at the northeast corner of Fish Creek Campground, near the lakeshore. Others must drive

Fisherman in Lake McDonald

past the campground entrance, then follow the gravel-surfaced Inside North Fork Road for 0.4 mile and park in the gravel pit on the left-hand side of the road (elevation 3280 feet).

The Hike: The trailhead is located 20 feet back down the road from the parking area, on the left. The trail descends through lodgepole forest to Fish Creek, then skirts the edge of the campground.

At 0.5 mile, a trail branches to the right, heading 0.3 mile to Rocky Point. This is a popular spot for fishermen and view seekers. It is also an excellent location to sit and watch the sunset.

The lake trail climbs over Rocky Point and continues in dense lodgepole forest until it descends to the lakeshore, and one of the few lakeshore viewpoints, at 1.8 miles.

The Lake McDonald backcountry campsite trail branches off on the right at 4.6 miles, providing an excellent turnaround point for day hikers.

The trail ends at 7 miles. From the trailhead it is 2.6 miles on a rough dirt road to the Lake McDonald Ranger Station and another 1.2 miles on a narrow paved road to the Going-to-the-Sun Road.

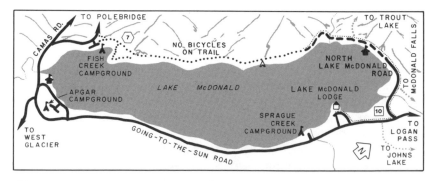

Logging Lake and Mount Geduhn

8 Logging Lake Trail

Round trip to Logging Lake: 10 miles (16 km)
Elevation gain: 387 feet (118 m)
High point: 3810 feet (1161 m)
Hiking time: 5 hours
Day hike or backpack

Round trip to Grace Lake: 25.6 miles (41 km)
Elevation gain: 577 feet (176 m)
High point: 4000 feet (1219 m)
Hiking time: 2–4 days
Backpack

This is a forested hike up the Logging Creek valley with little elevation gain. The trail spends most of its time near water, first paralleling Logging Creek, then traversing around Logging Lake. At the upper end of the lake, the trail once again parallels the creek along the forested valley floor to Grace Lake.

Because of its location on the west side of the park, the use of this trail by day hikers is relatively low. Backpackers, however, will find the three camp areas filled to capacity often during the summer months.

Access: The trailhead is reached by driving the narrow, rough, and winding Inside North Fork Road either 18 miles north from the Fish Creek Campground or 7.9 miles south from the Polebridge Ranger Station to Logging Creek.

The Hike: The trail starts out with a short climb, then levels off on a bench above Logging Creek. This is prime wildlife habitat. Deer and elk may be seen along the trail. Bears also frequent this area, so make plenty of noise, which will most likely also scare away the deer and elk.

The lower end of Logging Lake is reached at 4.4 miles. The trail divides here. Straight ahead, on a pretty peninsula, lies a patrol cabin and boat house with an excellent view up the lake to the Continental Divide. The peninsula is an ideal picnic and turnaround spot for day hikers.

Backpackers should continue up the lake. After another 0.2 mile the trail to the first campsite branches off on the right, descending 0.3 mile to the lakeshore. Adair Campground is reached at 9.4 miles from the road and, just 3.4 miles beyond, Grace Lake Campground marks the end of the official trail.

Although forested, Grace Lake is nearly surrounded by mountains: Logging Mountain, Vulture Peak, Nahsukin Mountain, Trapper Peak, Mount Geduhn, Anaconda Peak, and Wolf Gun Mountain. For those who wish to explore up the valley, fishermen have beaten paths along the shore of Grace Lake, but these trails are rough and soon disappear, leaving you to continue forth as the early trappers did, crawling over logs and beating through the brush.

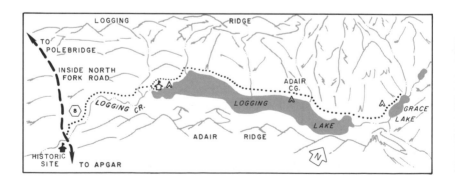

Bicycling

9 The Middle Fork Ride

Round trip: 8.6 miles (13.8 km)
Elevation gain: 180 feet (55 m)
High point: 3380 feet (1030 m)
Riding time: 1.5 hours
Surface: dirt and pavement
Difficulty: easy

Explore the lowland forest and the lesser-used byways on this fun and easy ride in the southwest corner of the park. This trip is excellent for people looking for a bit of evening exercise or for adven-

Forested road to Apgar Lookout trailhead

turous spirits who want to fill an entire day, combining bicycling with a hike to Apgar Lookout (see trip 1).

This is a ride designed for the entire family. The bike path and back roads followed on this route receive only minor use, and the terrain is mostly level with only a few short climbs that can easily be walked. You can even complete this trip on one of the Apgar rental bikes.

Access: The ride begins by following the bike path from the Apgar Campground. If you are not staying at Apgar, park your car near the campground entrance or at the picnic area. **(See map on page 40.)**

Log:

0.0 mile   Find the bike path near the campground entrance and follow it to Apgar Village. Ride with caution; this path is shared with pedestrians who will be moving at a slower speed than a cyclist.

0.3 mile   The path ends at Apgar Village. Go left on the road and head past the visitor center toward the Camas Road.

0.5 mile   Take a right onto the bike path.

0.7 mile   Cross the Camas Road. The Apgar Bridge to the right is a popular side trip. Park your bike on the bridge, then peer down into McDonald Creek and watch for fish. The bike path heads through dense lodgepole forest. Make plenty of noise as you ride to warn wildlife of your presence.

1.9 miles   Go right, leaving the bike path to follow a paved road.

2.2 miles   The road divides; stay right for 500 feet to the riding stables. The road expands into a large parking lot and several spur roads head toward the stable area. Ride through the parking area, then continue on a gravel road, following signs for Quarter Circle Bridge.

2.8 miles   Cross the Quarter Circle Bridge, a unique-looking structure located near the confluence of McDonald Creek and the Middle Fork Flathead River. Beyond the bridge, the road is rough but but very suitable for bicycles.

3.2 miles   The road begins to climb.

3.8 miles   Arrive at an intersection and go right toward the Apgar Lookout trailhead on a road that climbs steadily.

4.3 miles   The road ends in a small meadow. To the left, a gate marks the start of the Apgar Lookout Trail. Bicycles are not allowed beyond this point. If you are on a bike/hike, be sure to lock your bike before heading up the trail to the lookout. If you are looking for more riding, head back down the road for 0.5 mile to the intersection and follow the fire road on for 2.8 nearly level miles through the forest to the Flathead Ranger Station. This road is infrequently maintained, so expect a few branches or even downed trees in the road—a great adventure.

10 North Lake McDonald Road

Round trip: 9 miles (14.4 km)
Elevation gain: 100 feet (30 m)
High point: 3300 feet (1006 m)
Riding time: 2 hours
Surface: paved and dirt road
Difficulty: easy

Ride beneath a canopy of majestic Douglas fir and western red cedar on a narrow road around the north shore of Lake McDonald. Lucky riders may spot bears, deer, and even moose.

The North Lake McDonald Road was built to access the private dwellings along the lakeshore and a couple of trailheads. The road is paved for part of the distance and gravel for the remainder. It is extremely narrow—cars have a difficult time passing—and very rough: the ideal combination for a relaxing mountain bike tour.

The North Lake McDonald Road is short, so to extend the ride the starting point has been placed at Lake McDonald Lodge. This means that cyclists must brave the busy Going-to-the-Sun Road for 1.5 miles going and coming. To avoid the traffic, start your ride early (before 9:00 A.M.) or late (after 4:00 P.M.).

Access: From the West Entrance Station, drive the Going-to-the-Sun Road east for 10.2 miles to the Lake McDonald Lodge parking area. **(See map on page 54.)**

Log:

0.0 mile   Head east on the Going-to-the-Sun Road. There are no shoulders here, so ride with traffic as the road heads through forest over level terrain.

1.4 miles   Pass the Johns Lake Trail on the right.

1.5 miles   Turn left on the unsigned North Lake McDonald Road and descend to the bridge.

1.7 miles   Cross upper McDonald Creek. To the left is a view of Lake McDonald; to the right McDonald Falls can be seen.

1.8 miles   An unsigned trail parallels upper McDonald Creek to the falls.

1.9 miles   Reach the McDonald Creek trailhead; the trail wanders through the forest for 1 mile to Sacred Dancing Cascade. Beyond the trailhead, the road narrows and is full of potholes. On the left are several private homes.

2.3 miles   Pass the entrance to the Lake McDonald Ranger Station.

2.5 miles   The pavement ends. The road begins a series of short climbs and rolling descents.

Checking the map

3.1 miles The road widens slightly to provide a small parking area at the Trout Lake trailhead. A short distance beyond, pass a gate that is closed whenever the road is wet to reduce wear and tear in the soft soil.

4.5 miles Road's end at the Lake McDonald trailhead. The trail along the west side of the lake is closed to bicycles, so turn around and take a second look at the forest.

11 North Fork Loop

Loop trip: 59.4 miles (95 km)
Elevation gain: 2617 feet (798 m)
High point: 4200 feet (1280 m)
Riding time: 1–3 days
Surface: dirt and paved road
Difficulty: moderate

Ride the wild side of the park, where the pavement gives way to gravel and wildlife replaces the endless streams of people.

The wild side is the western edge of the park, which is bordered by the North Fork Flathead River. The river is in a broad valley, with the rugged, glacier-clad peaks of the park on the east and the forested Whitefish Range in the Flathead National Forest to the west. There is no paved road access to this area, leaving this side of the park delightfully primitive and ideal for cycling.

The North Fork Loop explores this area on roads inside and

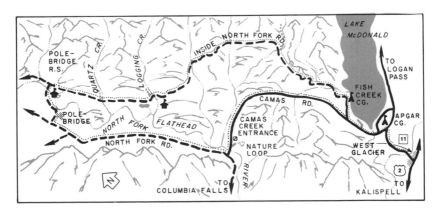

Black bear

outside of the park. The ride follows the Inside North Fork Road along the western park boundary. The road is rough, with steep climbs and bumpy descents—best suited for mountain or hybrid bikes. At Polebridge the loop leaves the park and turns south, following the gravel-surfaced North Fork Road back down the valley. The final section of the loop heads back into the park on the wide and smoothly paved Camas Road.

As befits a ride on the wild side of the park, there are few services. Only at the midpoint can you buy food. Lodging is available at the Polebridge Hostel (see the Where to Stay section in the Introduction) or you may camp at Bowman Lake, located 6 miles off the loop.

This is a loop for strong riders who enjoy bicycling for the pure thrill of turning the pedals. This is not a ride for anyone who is looking for grand vistas or easy cruising. The majority of the ride is through lodgepole forest where a lucky rider may see a deer, elk, or bear.

Access: The ride begins from the town of West Glacier. Leave your car in the large lot near the Alberta Visitor Center.

Log:

0.0 mile   West Glacier; stock up on food and liquid here, then head into Glacier National Park.

0.9 mile   Reach the Glacier National Park Entrance Station. The section of road ahead is busy, with minimal shoulder.

1.1 miles   A bicycle path crosses the road here. This path provides an excellent chance to escape the traffic, if you can safely make the left-hand turn to reach it. If not, continue straight.

2.1 miles   At a T intersection, go left.

2.4 miles   A road branches right to Apgar Village, the last chance for an ice cream cone for many miles.

2.5 miles   Bicycle path riders turn left onto the Camas Road just before crossing lower McDonald Creek. Just beyond the bridge the road divides; continue straight ahead.

2.7 miles   Begin a steep climb.

3.4 miles   Turn right toward Fish Creek Campground and descend to the shore of Lake McDonald.

4.4 miles   Reach the Fish Creek Campground entrance. Stay left when the road divides and head uphill on the gravel-surfaced Inside North Fork Road.

4.9 miles   Reach the Lake McDonald trailhead. A service road leads to the left; keep right.

6.4 miles   Pass the Howe Ridge Fire Trail; it's 9.4 miles of brushy hiking to reach the West Lakes Trail.

8.6 miles   At an elevation of 3920 feet, a brief descent marks the end of the longest climb on this loop.

10.1 miles The Howe Lake trailhead offers an easy 2-mile hike to a forested lake. The road begins a 1-mile-long descent.

11.4 miles Roll across Camas Creek, then pass the Camas Valley trailhead. The road makes a short climb, then descends into the next drainage.

14.4 miles Cross the Dutch Creek Bridge; the creek marks the entrance into a special preservation area. At certain times of year the next 8 miles must be ridden without stopping. The road climbs as it leaves the Dutch Creek drainage, then descends the steep Anaconda Hill grade.

17.1 miles Reach Anaconda Creek; the descent continues, but at a more gradual pace.

20.9 miles   Ride around the west side of Sullivan Meadows, then descend a bit more.

22.3 miles   Arrive at the Logging Creek Ranger Station and the end of the preservation area. Take a break, stop and read the sign describing the old ranger station, and have a picnic in the overgrown campground.

22.4 miles   Reach Logging Creek and the Logging Creek trailhead (elevation 3437 feet).

23.9 miles   A short, steep descent ends at the edge of the North Fork Flathead River. Stop and enjoy the view.

24.7 miles   Pass the site of the old Quartz Creek Campground.

25.0 miles   Pass the Quartz Creek trailhead; it is 6.1 miles to Lower Quartz Lake.

25.4 miles   The road passes Winona Lake, then makes a short, steep climb into forest burnt by the 1988 Red Bench fire.

27.0 miles   Enter Lone Pine Prairie.

27.1 miles   Pass the Hidden Meadow Trail, a short hike with a good chance to view wildlife.

30.3 miles   The road divides. To the right the road continues on for 6 miles to Bowman Lake and 15 miles to Kintla Lake. For the loop route, go left toward the Polebridge Entrance Station, the town, and the hostel.

30.4 miles   Cross the North Fork of the Flathead River on a wide bridge, built after the 1988 fire.

31.8 miles   Reach the Polebridge Mercantile and a small eatery. The road divides here. The Polebridge Hostel is to the left; the loop route takes the right fork.

32.1 miles   Go left on the North Fork Road and head down the valley. This is a two-lane gravel road, with potholes and lots of washboard. Traffic is heavier on this road, dust is thicker, and the scenery is much better.

33.2 miles   The Hay Creek Bridge marks the start of a 5.4-mile section of nearly level paved road.

36.4 miles   Reach the Home Ranch Store, with snacks, showers, and cabins.

38.6 miles   The pavement ends.

45.3 miles   Reach an intersection; go left on a paved road.

45.9 miles   A road on the right leads to a self-guided nature trail. This atypical trail is steep, rough, and interesting, if you are unfamiliar with ecotones (ecologic transition areas).

46.2 miles   Pass the Camas Entrance Station. The wide, shoulder-less road continues its gradual climb.

48.8 miles   The Camas Creek Overlook has an interesting wolf exhibit.

51.3 miles   Pass the Huckleberry Lookout trailhead. The trail climbs 6 miles through the berry fields to the lookout. This area is closed in late summer due to bears.

51.5 miles   Reach McGee Meadow, a good place to watch for wildlife.

53.8 miles   After crossing Fern Creek the road descends.

55.9 miles   Pass the turnoff to Fish Creek Campground. Continue the descent.

59.4 miles   The loop ends where it started, in the parking lot at West Glacier.

Downtown Polebridge

12 Going-To-The-Sun Road

One way from West Glacier to St. Mary: 51.2 miles (82 km)
Elevation gain: 3527 feet (1075 m)
High point: 6680 feet (2036 m)
Riding time: 6 hours
Surface: narrow, paved road
Difficulty: moderate

Round trip to Logan Pass from Lake McDonald Lodge: 43 miles
   (69 km)
Riding time: 5½ hours

Names like Weeping Wall, Garden Wall, Hanging Gardens, and Going-to-the-Sun help to explain the popularity of the difficult ride over Logan Pass.

The Going-to-the-Sun Road over Logan Pass is better suited for bicycles than cars. The blind corners, the sharp twists, and the narrow roadway (which cause so much trouble for motorists), all combine to create a bicycling paradise. The slow pace of a climbing cyclist is perfect for contemplating mountains like Heavens Peak, Heavy Runner, and Almost a Dog.

It is a long, slow grind up to Logan Pass, but the descent is a breeze, with only the motor vehicles to slow you down. Because some drivers on this road behave in an erratic fashion, paying more attention to the scenery than to their driving, avoid tailgating any slowly descending vehicles.

Due to the popularity of this road and to ensure the steady flow of motor vehicle traffic, the Park Service has enacted strict regulations concerning cycling. From June 15 through Labor Day, two sections of the Going-to-the-Sun Road are closed to bicycles from 11:00 A.M. to 4:00 P.M. These sections are the 7.4 miles around Lake McDonald from Apgar Campground to Sprague Creek Campground and the 11.4-mile climb from Logan Creek to Logan Pass. The entire east side, from Logan Pass to St. Mary, is open all day.

Each of the five campgrounds along the Going-to-the-Sun Road have hiker/biker sites. These sites are reserved for cyclists, hikers, and motorcyclists until 9:00 P.M. every night. Each site can hold up to eight people; the cost is on a per person basis.

The mileage log below tracks the ride from west to east, the most commonly ridden direction. However, if you have the option, ride from east to west. The ride from St. Mary to Logan Pass is shorter, with an elevation gain that is 1331 feet less than the west side's.

As you ride the Going-to-the-Sun Road, you will see signs with numbers on them. These signs are part of a geological tour and denote points of interest. In order to understand this tour you must buy a book, available at the visitor center.

If you decide to ride to Logan Pass and back in a day, you must either start early in the morning or take enough supplies to spend the day at the top and ride back in the evening. For round-trip riders, Lake McDonald Lodge is a popular starting point.

Access: This ride description begins from the town of West Glacier at the intersection of Highway 2 and the Going-to-the-Sun Road. Drive, or ride, under the railroad tracks and park in the large lot on the left (elevation 3215 feet).

Log:

0.0 mile   West Glacier; all tourist facilities are available here except camping. There is a grocery store, a post office, a bar, a camera store, a restaurant, rafting companies, souvenirs, and a laundromat.

0.9 mile   Reach the West Entrance Station; pay your fee, receive a map, and ask questions.

1.1 miles   A bike path to Apgar crosses the road here.

2.0 miles   At a T intersection, go right.

2.8 miles   Reach an intersection; a left turn leads to Apgar Campground, a picnic area, the visitor center, motels, a grocery store, a cafe, souvenirs, and rest rooms. The Going-to-the-Sun Road continues straight, entering the first of the two restricted areas as it parallels the south shore of Lake McDonald. There are plenty of pullouts and gravel beaches along the lake, all on the left side of the road.

3.4 miles   An exhibit on the left explains the glacial origins of Lake McDonald.

9.7 miles   Pass the Lincoln Lake trailhead, on the right. It's a long forest hike to a scenic lake and a waterfall.

10.2 miles Pass the Sprague Creek Campground to the left, with rest rooms and running water. This is a pleasant lakeside camp area designed for tent camping.

10.6 miles An exhibit on the left explains the history of Indians and settlers at Lake McDonald.

11.1 miles Pass Lake McDonald Lodge on the left, with rest rooms, water, a cafe, a small store, riding stables, lake tours, and the Gunsight Pass trailhead.

12.4 miles The Sacred Dancing Cascade Loop Trail crosses the road.

12.6 miles Reach an intersection; the unsigned North Lake McDonald Road branches to the left.

12.8 miles McDonald Falls can be seen from the pullout on the left.

13.2 miles The Johns Lake Trail, on the right, leads to a shallow, forested lake. To the left is an overlook of the Sacred Dancing Cascade.

13.9 miles Pass a small pond and an exhibit on the right where moose are occasionally seen.

14.7 miles The Upper McDonald Falls viewpoint on the left. It is worth the stop.

16.6 miles Avalanche Campground and Avalanche Lake trailhead are on the right and a picnic area is on the left; water and rest rooms are available.

16.7 miles Trail of the Cedars is a short nature trail through a grove of large western red cedars.

18.9 miles An exhibit on the right explains the damage caused by avalanches.

20.8 miles Rest rooms are on the right.

21.2 miles Reach Logan Creek (elevation 3550 feet), the start of the second restricted section. The climb to the pass begins here.

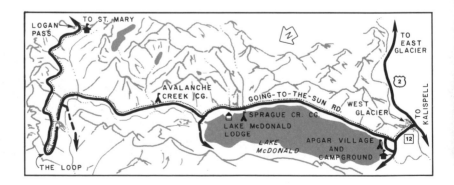

Cyclists at Logan Pass on Going-to-the-Sun Road

McDonald Creek valley viewed from Going-to-the-Sun Road

24.0 miles Go through a short tunnel with a waterfall at the upper end.

24.7 miles Reach the Loop; a parking area, exhibits, and the Granite Park trailhead are located here. From this point on, the road is narrow, blasted into the rock wall. All turnouts and exhibits are now located on the right.

27.5 miles Bird Woman Falls Overlook.

29.5 miles The Weeping Wall; water pours off the hillside in the early summer.

29.8 miles A geology exhibit.

32.1 miles Switchback; you are very close to the top now.

32.6 miles The 6680-foot summit of Logan Pass and the Continental Divide. The visitor center has water, rest rooms, displays, and a bookstore. If time allows, take a short hike

through the Hanging Gardens to the Hidden Lake Overlook before heading down to St. Mary.

34.1 miles A tunnel and two waterfalls make this a popular stopping point for cars and buses.

35.6 miles Siyeh Bend, with a geology exhibit and a trailhead. The
steep descent continues with distracting views.

37.5 miles Jackson Glacier Photographic Point is an excellent
viewpoint as well as a trailhead for Gunsight Pass.

38.2 miles A viewpoint and an exhibit discussing avalanches.

39.7 miles The St. Mary Falls trailhead; it's only 1 mile to the falls.

40.4 miles Sunrift Gorge; a short walk leads to an amazingly deep
and narrow gorge.

41.0 miles The Sun Point turnoff is on the right. A short descent
leads to a picnic area, an outhouse, and a short nature
trail along the shore of St. Mary Lake.

44.0 miles Wild Goose Island Photographic Point on the right. Everyone stops for a look, so join the crowd.

44.7 miles Boat tours on the right.

44.8 miles Rising Sun Campground, with a motel, a general store,
showers, and a cafeteria to the left. At 4484 feet, this is
the end of the descent. The road is nearly level as it follows the shoreline of the lake to St. Mary.

46.7 miles The Triple Divide Peak Overlook is on the right.

50.4 miles St. Mary Campground is on the left, with water and rest
rooms.

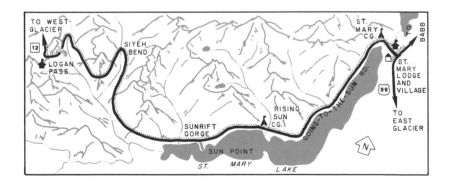

St. Mary Lake

50.6 miles St. Mary Entrance Station and the visitor center is on the left, with displays, a park movie, information, maps, books, water, and rest rooms.

50.9 miles Pass the turnoff to the Red Eagle Lake Trail and the historic 1913 Ranger Station.

51.2 miles St. Mary Village, with a store, a post office, a laundromat, a cafe, souvenirs, a motel, and buffalo burgers.

POLEBRIDGE

Polebridge is a small, isolated community located on the west side of Glacier National Park in the North Fork Flathead River valley. It is isolated by geography, boxed in by mountain ranges to the east and west. It is isolated by distance; the nearest city is Columbia Falls, located 41 miles to the south. It is isolated by roads that are dirt and often very rough for driving. And it is isolated by design, because the residents like it that way.

During the summer months there are three ways to drive to Polebridge. The partially paved North Fork Road may be driven all the way from Columbia Falls. The narrow and very rough Inside North Fork Road may be followed from Fish Creek Campground. However, the easiest access is to drive the paved Camas Road from Apgar for half the distance, then complete the second half of the trip on the rough gravel of the North Fork Road.

Accommodations And Services

Lodging in Polebridge is limited to a small number of cabins near the Mercantile and the hostel. The hostel is popular and usually booked for months in advance. It has a kitchen, and guests do their own cooking or have a meal at the small restaurant next to the Mercantile. Electricity is not available in Polebridge, so lights, stoves, and refrigerators run off kerosene or propane. Mountain bikes and some backpacking equipment may be rented at the hostel. Transportation to Polebridge can be arranged to and from the West Glacier (Belton) train station in West Glacier. Write to the North Fork Hostel, Polebridge, MT 59928, or phone (406) 756-4780 for reservations and information.

The Polebridge Mercantile is an old store with a good supply of knickknacks and some food. Regular gas is available.

Inside the park, facilities include a forty-eight-site campground at Bowman Lake and a picnic area. The access road to the lake is very narrow, and trailers or long RVs are not advised. The toilets are the vault type.

Bowman Lake

There is also a thirteen-site campground at Kintla Lake that offers a vault toilet and running water. Trailers and RVs will have a hard time on the narrow Kintla Lake Road and are not recommended.

At Big Creek, just south of the Camas Entrance, there is a Flathead National Forest campground. No private campgrounds or trailer facilities are available in the Polebridge area.

Activities

Boating and fishing on Kintla and Bowman lakes are the most popular activities on the west side of Glacier National Park. No motors are allowed on Kintla Lake, making it the best lake in the park for canoeing or kayaking. The backcountry campground at the head of Kintla Lake is an ideal destination. Bowman Lake is open to small motors, 10 hp or less, and has a boat ramp. Both lakes are subject to sudden strong winds, so small boats should stay close to shore at all times.

Canoeing and rafting are popular activities on the Wild and Scenic North Fork Flathead River from Polebridge to Big Creek Campground. The only hazards on this section of river are submerged logs and log jams.

Mountain biking is a popular sport on the dirt roads in the park and on the forest roads outside the park. This chapter includes two suggested rides.

Short Hikes

Hidden Meadow. A 1.5-mile round trip leads to a meadow and two small lakes. This is a great place to spot deer, elk, and occasion-

Canoeing on Kintla Lake

ally bears. The trailhead is located on the Inside North Fork Road, 3.2 miles south of the Polebridge Entrance Station.

Day Hikes And Backpacks

13 Bowman Lake

Round trip to Bowman Lake Campground: 13.6 miles (22 km)
Elevation gain: 100 feet (30 m)
High point: 4030 feet (1228 m)
Hiking time: 7 hours
Day hike or backpack

Round trip to Brown Pass: 27.6 miles (44.2 km)
Elevation gain: 2225 feet (678 m)
High point: 6255 feet (1906 m)
Hiking time: 2–3 days
Backpack

Fjordlike Bowman Lake is a narrow, 7-mile-long finger of water boxed in by steep mountains. This is a beautiful setting for a family stroll, an easy backpack, or an extended journey up the Bowman Creek valley to the Continental Divide and the alpine meadows at Brown Pass.

If you are planning an overnight trip, it is best to obtain your permits at the Apgar Visitor Center before heading north to Pole-

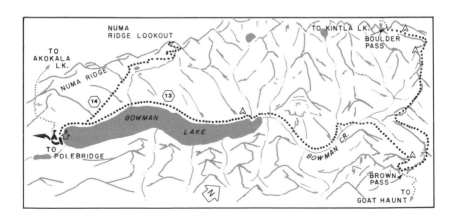

Bowman Lake

bridge. Permits are also issued at the Polebridge Ranger Station—
but only when someone is available to do it.

Access: From West Glacier, drive the Camas Road 14 miles to
the North Fork Road and turn right. The road is rough and mostly
gravel for the next 13.2 miles. At the Polebridge intersection, turn
right and drive 1.7 miles to the Polebridge Entrance and Ranger
Station. Go left on the Inside North Fork Road, drive 0.1 mile, then
turn right on the rough and very narrow Bowman Lake Road. After
6 miles the road ends. Park in the hikers' area, next to the picnic
ground (elevation 4030 feet).

The Hike: The trail begins at the boat launching area and
heads north, around the end of the lake. Pass the ranger's residence, then head into the forest. At 0.7 mile a trail branches left to
Numa Ridge Lookout (see trip 14). Stay right.

As you head up the lake, Rainbow Peak, Mount Carter, and
Thunderbird Mountain come into view to the southeast. Near the

head of the lake, at 6.8 miles, you pass a backcountry camp area. This is the turnaround point for day hikers and an overnight stop for backpackers.

Beyond the lake, the trail heads through forest, up the swampy Bowman Creek valley for 3 miles before beginning a long climb across the lower flanks of Chapman Peak. Near the top, the trail leaves the forest, providing an opportunity for views to the west.

A waterfall marks the entrance to the basin just below the pass. Shortly beyond, at 13.5 miles from the trailhead, is the Brown Pass backcountry campsite. Then it's 0.3 mile of relatively easy walking to 6255-foot Brown Pass, where the Bowman Lake Trail meets the Boulder Pass Trail and ends. Take advantage of any spare time to do some high-country exploring of the exquisite alpine meadows at Hole-in-the-Wall and Boulder Pass. If a shuttle car is available, try the excellent hike from Brown Pass to Kintla Lake (see trip 16).

14 Numa Ridge Lookout

Round trip: 11.4 miles (18 km)
Elevation gain: 2930 feet (1523 m)
High point: 6960 feet (2744 m)
Hiking time: 6 hours
Day hike

A view that encompasses the magnificent grandeur of the glacier-carved Bowman Valley, the jade-colored waters of Bowman Lake, the massive Rainbow, Square, and Carter mountains to the east, and the broad North Fork Flathead River valley and forested Whitefish Range to the west is the reward for the long climb to the Numa Ridge Lookout.

The trail to this magnificent view is well graded, allowing for a gradual climb from the shores of the lake to the lookout. Be sure to carry plenty of water; the ridge is dry.

Access: Drive to Bowman Lake **(see map on page 76).**

The Hike: Follow the Bowman Lake Trail from the boat launch area, pass the ranger station, and continue along the northwest shore of the lake for 0.7 mile to a junction. Go left on the Numa Ridge Trail and head uphill. The climb is gradual, and the trail gains only 1000 feet in the next 2.8 miles.

Hiker near crest of Numa Ridge

At 3.5 miles there is a short descent into a wooded basin (elevation 5120 feet) where a small, nameless pond is hidden in the trees on the right.

The trail begins to climb with a bit more determination, heading to the open meadows and views. Before long, Bowman Lake can be seen as well as forested Cerulean Ridge. To the west, north, and south are the minor and major summits of the Whitefish Range.

The lookout is located on a 6960-foot crest of a minor bump on Numa Ridge. The building is occupied during times of high fire danger at the end of the summer. Hikers may walk up the stairs and wander around the balcony, which is a great place to scan the open hillsides for wildlife. In late summer, look for bears grazing on the huckleberries in the basin below.

Patrol cabin at Quartz Lake

15 Quartz Lakes Loop

Loop trip: 12.8 miles (20.5 km)
Elevation gain: 2279 feet (695 m)
High point: 5400 feet (1646 m)
Hiking time: 7 hours
Day hike or backpack

This is a loop hike to the three Quartz Lakes. The lakes are forested, views are minimal, but fishing for cutthroat is a popular activity. Serious fishermen can make a good catch from the lakeshore; those who need to nudge Lady Luck a little should add a small raft or belly float to their packs.

There are two backcountry campgrounds for those who do not choose to race around the loop in a single day. The lakeside camp area at Quartz Lake is recommended for the view you will have from your tent door; however, no fires are allowed. Campsites at Lower Quartz Lake are sheltered in the trees and fires are permitted there.

If you plan to overnight on the trail, obtain your permit from the Apgar Visitor Center before heading north.

Access: Drive to Bowman Lake (see trip 13 for directions) and leave your car in the hikers' parking area (elevation 4030 feet).

The Hike: Walk to the shore of Bowman Lake, then turn right and head south on the trail, crossing a footbridge over the outlet and passing a ranger's residence. At 0.4 mile the trail leaves the lakeshore and divides, marking the start of the loop.

The loop may be hiked in either direction. This trip description begins with the right fork in order to complete the steep portion of the trail early in the day. Backpackers may prefer the meandering style of the left fork which allows for a gradual climb over Cerulean Ridge.

Heading right, the trail climbs over 5100-foot Cerulean Ridge and drops to Lower Quartz Lake in just 3.1 miles. The climb is steep and rough and never bothers with any unnecessary rambling. At the top of the ridge, take time to enjoy the view over the Quartz Creek Valley before descending straight down through the burn of 1988 to Lower Quartz Lake (elevation 4191 feet).

On the east side of Quartz Creek, in the middle of the camp cooking area, the trail divides. The right fork is a rarely used trail that descends 6.9 miles to the Inside North Fork Road.

The loop trail heads up the valley, and at 6 miles 4397-foot Middle Quartz Lake comes into view. Shortly beyond, the trail recrosses Quartz Creek, then climbs a small rise and descends to

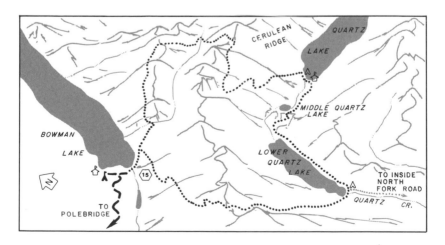

Quartz Lake. A patrol cabin is passed before the trail reaches the camp area at 6.6 miles (elevation 4416 feet).

Leaving Quartz Lake, the loop route heads back up to the crest of Cerulean Ridge. Once on top, the trail begins to wander, making a complete tour of the forested hillside before descending to the start at Bowman Lake.

16 Kintla Lake and the Boulder Pass Trail

Round trip to Kintla Lake camp: 12.6 miles (21 km)
Elevation gain: 160 feet (49 m)
High point: 4160 feet (1268 m)
Hiking time: 6 hours
Day hike or backpack

Round trip to Boulder Pass: 35.4 miles (57 km)
Elevation gain: 3462 feet (1055 m)
High point: 7470 feet (2277 m)
Hiking time: 3–4 days
Backpack

Boulder Pass is one of the favorite backcountry areas of Glacier National Park hikers. As it is hard to describe the area without tripping over an endless string of superlatives, let it suffice to say that the meadows and rocky summits make the long hike worthwhile.

The ideal way to hike the Boulder Pass Trail is to follow it all

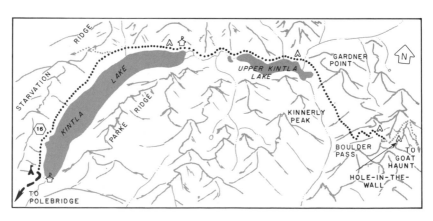

Hiker near camp area at upper end of Kintla Lake

the way from Kintla Lake to Goat Haunt at the upper end of Waterton Lake. However, for most people, even those with two vehicles at their disposal, the transportation logistics are too difficult and time-consuming. Most hikers find it easier to establish a base camp at Boulder Pass and spend a day or more exploring.

Access: Arrange your backcountry permits at the Apgar Visitor Center, then drive to Polebridge. Once in the park, turn left on the Inside North Fork Road and drive 14.7 miles to road's end at Kintla Lake. The road is narrow and some sections are rough, so allow plenty of time for the drive. Dayhikers park in the special area near the lake; backpackers must leave their cars at the overnight parking area at the west side of the campground (elevation 4015 feet).

The Hike: Unlike many of the other popular trails in the park,

Golden-mantled ground squirrel

this one has retained its rustic feel with roots and rocks in the narrow track. The result is a trail with a real wilderness flavor.

At the upper end of Kintla Lake, 6.3 miles from the start, the trail passes through a backcountry camp area, scenically located near the lakeshore, with views of Kinnerly Peak and Boundary Mountain. Just 0.2 mile beyond, a patrol cabin at the end of the lake marks the start of a 2.5-mile forest walk to Upper Kintla Lake.

The trail skirts around Upper Kintla Lake for 2 miles and passes a backcountry campsite near the upper end. Beyond the lake, it's time to grit your teeth for the 5-mile climb to the pass. The trail is steep and very warm in the afternoon heat. At 5200 feet the switchbacks begin, and the climb is relentless until the trail reaches a high bench at 7200 feet. When the climb tapers off, the trail heads through a beautiful larch forest, which is replaced by open meadows at the pass.

The Boulder Pass camp area is located 17.2 miles from the start, and just 0.5 mile beyond is 7470-foot Boulder Pass. If you have a good map and compass, it is fun to explore the small tarns below Gardener Point, look for the colorful boulder fields on the ridge crest above the pass, or stroll down to Hole-in-the-Wall.

Bicycling

17 Bowman Lake

Round trip: 11.8 miles (18.9 km)
Elevation gain: 750 feet in (229 m); 120 feet out (37 m)
High point: 4080 feet (1244 m)
Riding time: 3 hours
Surface: dirt and gravel road
Difficulty: moderate

More than half of this fascinating tour is spent riding through the 1988 Red Bench Burn. The regrowth in the burn has been phenomenal, and hillsides are covered with grass, fireweed, and a seedling forest. White-tailed deer are flourishing on the verdant new growth; it is an unlucky cyclist who does not see at least one. Bears and elk also forage for food on these hillsides, but are less likely to be spotted. The second half of the ride is through the cool shade of a mature forest, a sharp contrast to the open hillsides of the burn area.

The ride to Bowman Lake is short, but by no means easy. The road surface is rough, with rocks, washboard, and potholes. The climbs are very steep, but luckily quite short.

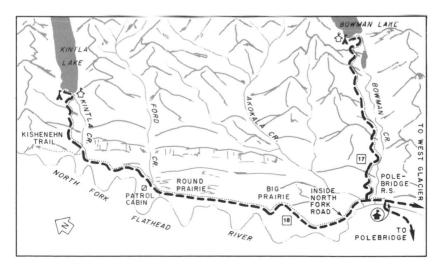

Stormy day at Bowman Lake

Motor vehicle traffic on this road is usually light and slow moving. This is not a problem on the way up, but on the way out the cars will be moving more slowly than the bikes. If you decide to pass, use a great deal of caution.

In 1992 the water at Bowman Lake Campground was not potable, so carry all you will need with you.

Access: From West Glacier, drive the Camas Road for 14 miles to the North Fork Flathead Road. Turn right and head up the valley for a rough and very bumpy 13.2 miles. Turn right at the small town of Polebridge and drive 1.7 miles to the park entrance. Park here (elevation 3600 feet).

Log:

0.0 mile   Head uphill for 100 feet from the entrance station to an intersection with the Inside North Fork Road. Go left, following the signs for Bowman Lake.

0.2 mile   Cross Bowman Creek. Just ahead, on the right, is an exhibit discussing the Red Bench Fire.

0.3 mile   At the intersection, go right on the Bowman Lake Road and immediately start to climb.

1.1 miles   The road makes a short, steep descent to the edge of

Bowman Creek, then returns to the business of climbing.

2.5 miles   At the top of this hill the Livingston Range comes into view.

3.1 miles   Leave the burn area and enter the forest. The change is immediate; different wildflowers and different birds inhabit this side of the hill. The road makes several short, steep climbs as it heads over rolling terrain.

5.4 miles   A meadow on the left side of the road marks the start of the final descent to the lake.

5.8 miles   Pass the public horse ramp on the right.

5.9 miles   Reach Bowman Lake (elevation 4030 feet). The campground is located on the left and the picnic area is on the right. The boat ramp and trailheads are straight ahead at the lakeshore. Bowman Lake is cradled between Cerulean Ridge on the right and Numa Ridge on the left, with Numa, Square, and Rainbow peaks spiking the horizon at the head of the lake.

18 Kintla Lake

Round trip: 29.4 miles (47.2 km)
Elevation gain: 700 feet in (213 m); 200 feet out (37 m)
High point: 4300 feet (1311 m)
Riding time: 6 hours
Surface: dirt and gravel road
Difficulty: easy

Miles of open prairie with a backdrop of rugged mountains, groves of aspen, birch, and lodgepole forest, and a lake that looks like a Norwegian fjord combine to make this tour a photographer's dream.

Despite the considerable distance involved, the ride is rated as easy. The road surface is solid with relatively few potholes (except after a rainstorm), and the elevation gain is minimal. No supplies are available along the route, so carry enough food and water to last the entire day.

Access: Park at the Polebridge Ranger Station (see trip 17 for directions; **see map on page 85**).

Log:

0.0 mile   From the parking area at the entrance station, ride up-

Round Prairie on Inside North Fork Road

hill for 100 feet to an intersection with the Inside North Fork Road. Go left following the Kintla Lake signs.

0.2 mile   Cross Bowman Creek. Just ahead is an exhibit explaining the effect of the 1988 Red Bench Fire. As you pedal on through the burn area, watch for white-tailed deer feeding on the new growth.

0.3 mile   Continue straight at the intersection with the Bowman Lake Road.

2.0 miles   Enter Big Prairie, a large grassland with only an occasional grove of trees to interrupt your view. To the east, Reuter and Parke peaks dominate the horizon; to the west lie the forested foothills of the Whitefish Range.

2.6 miles   Pass several privately owned ranch houses, left over from the days before this area was part of Glacier National Park.

6.5 miles   Big Prairie ends. The road makes a short climb, passing a gate near the top. Over the next mile, several river access roads branch off to the left.

7.7 miles   Enter Round Prairie. In autumn the birch and aspen trees to the east shimmer with an effervescent gold.

8.2 miles   Leave Round Prairie. At this point the road heads into the forest, where it rolls over low ridges with occasional short, but steep, climbs.

8.8 miles   Cross Ford Creek, then cycle past a patrol cabin.

12.0 miles A river access road branches off to the left, and the Kintla Lake Road turns east to parallel Kintla Creek.

12.4 miles Cross Kintla Creek and begin the final climb.

12.7 miles To the left, the Kishenehn Trail up the North Fork Flathead River starts off following an old road.

13.4 miles The climb ends on top of an ancient terminal moraine.

14.7 miles The road ends at Kintla Lake Campground; pit toilets and water are available. Take your time, picnic on the lakeshore, and absorb the view.

WALTON

Walton lies at the forgotten, southern corner of Glacier National Park, near the small town of Essex. Civilization's main encroachments in this narrow section of the Middle Fork Flathead River valley are Highway 2 and the Burlington Northern railroad tracks. On the north side of the valley, the pristine wilderness of Glacier National Park begins a few feet from the road; to the south, the Great Bear and Bob Marshall wilderness areas preserve a huge tract of the Rocky Mountains along the crest of the Continental Divide.

Accommodations And Services

The only service offered by the park in this area is a small picnic area located next to the Walton Ranger Station. It has picnic tables and pit toilets. There is no park lodging or camping here.

The nearest overnight accommodations are found at the Izaak Walton Inn in Essex. The inn is located next to the railroad tracks

Viewing platform at Goat Lick

and has a railroad theme to the buildings. Guests may stay in the inn or in remodeled cabooses. Other motels are located a few miles to the west on Highway 2. Private campgrounds are located to the east and west of Walton.

Activities

The Goat Lick is the most popular attraction in this area. Located 1.7 miles east of the Walton Ranger Station on the south side of Highway 2, it is a unique area where the mountain goats come down from the ridge tops, traveling for miles to lick mineral deposits. As many as fifty animals have been seen at the lick at one time. The best time for viewing is in the spring or early summer, during the mornings or late afternoons.

Short Hikes

Ole Creek. This is a 1-mile round-trip hike to Ole Creek and a delta at its confluence with the Middle Fork Flathead River. The trail begins at the Walton Picnic Area and wanders through the forest to the creek. Walk across the suspension bridge, then leave the main trail and follow an unmarked path to the river.

Day Hikes and Backpacks

19 Scalplock Mountain Lookout

Round trip: 9 miles (14.4 km)
Elevation gain: 3199 feet (975 m)
High point: 6919 feet (2109 m)
Hiking time: 6 hours
Day hike

The best viewpoint at the southern end of the park is found on the summit of Scalplock Mountain. Anyone visiting the summit for the first time is advised to carry a detailed map to help with the identification of the mountains and valleys that radiate out from Scalplock Mountain like spokes from a wheel.

Taking advantage of the superb view, a fire lookout tower has been built on the summit of the mountain and is staffed in times of extreme fire danger. However, most of the summer the trail and summit are quiet, ignored by the majority of park visitors.

Access: From West Glacier, drive Highway 2 east for 26.5

Mother and son enjoying view at summit of Scalplock Mountain

miles. Cross the Middle Fork Flathead River Bridge, then turn left to the Walton Ranger Station and Picnic Area. Leave your car in the small backcountry parking area (elevation 3720 feet). Be sure to carry a good supply of water; the climb to the summit is long, steep, and very dry.

The Hike: From the picnic area, the trail heads down the forested valley for 0.4 mile to Ole Creek. Once the creek is crossed on a very springy suspension bridge, the trail begins to climb the steep hillside.

The first intersection is reached at 1 mile. Take the left fork. At 1.3 miles the trail divides for the second and last time. Take the right fork and begin the climb up Scalplock with the first of many switchbacks.

Most of the hike is in the forest; however, occasional openings provide fascinating views of the Middle Fork Flathead River valley, the community of Essex, and the Flathead Range. As you continue up the steep hillside, watch the trains come and go through the Essex switching yard, adding engines for the climb over Marias Pass or unhooking them in preparation for the next eastbound train.

An open ridge is reached at 3.7 miles, and for the first time on this hike the views extend to the east over the Ole Creek valley, into the heart of the park. The trail ends at 4.5 miles, on the crest of the 6919-foot summit of Scalplock Mountain.

Now is the time to spread out the map and locate the places you have visited and the places you would like to hike to before you leave the park. Don't ignore the Flathead Range to the southwest. It is easy to see that there is plenty of beautiful country to explore beyond the borders of the park.

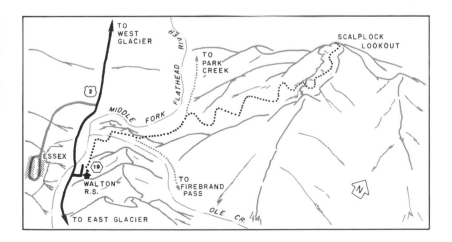

20 Nyack–Coal Creek Wilderness Camping Zone

Loop trip: 39.9 miles (63.8 km)
Elevation gain: 2590 feet (789 m)
High point: 6090 feet (1856 m)
Hiking time: 4–6 days
Backpack

If you came to Glacier National Park seeking solitude and true wilderness, this is the hike for you. Most of the trip is through forested valley bottoms with none of the high mountain vistas that draw hikers by the thousands to other areas of the park. The trails are rough, fallen trees may lie for months before they are cleared, brush may obscure the path, and bridges, for the most part, are nonexistent.

To start the hike, the Middle Fork Flathead River must be forded. Hikers and horses alike will have trouble with the crossing in early summer. Hikers should wait until at least late August before attempting the ford.

This is the only area in the park where hikers are not required to camp in designated areas. The four campsites on the loop are for parties with stock or for anyone planning to have a campfire. Hikers who are wilderness camping must carry a stove and use low-impact techniques. It is also extremely important to follow all the

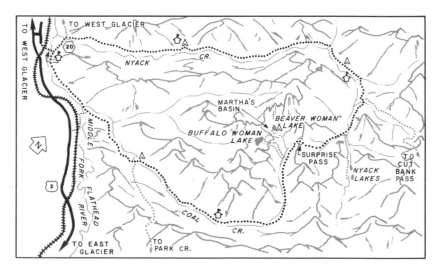

Hiker fording Middle Fork Flathead River in September

rules pertaining to hiking and camping in bear country, such as hanging food and cooking well away from the sleeping area.

(Note: Backcountry permits are required, even if you are not camping in a designated area. When picking up a backcountry permit, get the Nyack Trailhead map, which shows the ford area in detail.)

Access: Drive Highway 2 east for 10.9 miles from West Glacier. Turn left on a gravel road and head north 0.2 mile to a T intersection. Turn right, passing a hitching rail, and park off the road in the meadow (elevation 3351 feet).

The Hike: Walk the old road along the edge of the tracks. When the road ends, cross the tracks and find an obscure trail on the opposite side that heads through the cottonwoods to the river. Walk across the gravel bar to the river's edge. Looking across, find the place on the opposite shore where the gravel bar meets a grassy bank. Head straight across at this point. On the north side, the trail crosses a grassy area and an old river channel before reaching the official trail sign.

Just beyond the site of the old Nyack Ranger Station, intersect the South Boundary Trail and go left, downstream, for 0.7 mile to the Nyack Creek Trail, then turn right and head up the Nyack Creek valley. At 7.2 miles from the Middle Fork ford, the trail passes a patrol cabin. The valley bottom narrows, then widens, and the views improve as the trail heads into the mountains. A second patrol cabin is passed at 15.3 miles. At 16.9 miles, the trail to Cut Bank and Pitamakan passes heads off to the east. Leave the Nyack Creek Trail at 19.1 miles (elevation 4800 feet), and begin to climb on the Surprise Pass Trail.

It takes 2.5 miles of steady climbing to reach 5900-foot Surprise Pass. The trail then descends to meet the Coal Creek Trail, 21.6 miles from the Middle Fork. The loop route heads left, down Coal Creek. The right fork heads up into Martha's Basin to two subalpine lakes, well worth the 1.4-mile side trip.

The Coal Creek Trail descends, passing an intersection with the Fielding Creek Trail at 30.4 miles from the Middle Fork and ending at the South Boundary Trail at 36.1 miles. Head west for a final 3.8 miles to complete the loop at the old Nyack Ranger Station.

Missing from this description is a discussion of the many creek crossings encountered on the loop. It is recommended that you check current conditions of the creek crossings at the Apgar Visitor Center before starting the hike.

TWO MEDICINE AND EAST GLACIER PARK

The Two Medicine area is considered by many visitors to be the most scenic part of the park. However, no matter which portion of the park you pick as your favorite, this area with its many outstanding vista points and excellent walks should not be missed.

It is worth noting that Two Medicine is the only major park access that does not have a lodge. Accommodations for this area are located outside the park boundary in the town of East Glacier Park.

Accommodations And Services

The most important feature of East Glacier Park is the Amtrak station. Visitors arriving by train can arrange for a rental car to be waiting at the station or they can be picked up by a Red Bus and whisked the 0.1 mile over to the Glacier Park Lodge.

If the lodge is not in your price range, try one of several motels or the Youth Hostel (called Brownies Grocery and Hostel). Food is

Two Medicine area viewed from Highway 49

Two Medicine Lake

not a problem either; there are several restaurants, fast food outlets, and a small general store. The lodge offers such amenities as a golf course and several lowland hikes.

If you need transportation around the park, arrange your tour with Glacier Park, Inc. at the lodge.

Two Medicine has a large campground, including a hiker/biker area with food storage boxes for campers without vehicles. The campground is often full by midafternoon during the summer months. If you arrive late in the day, try the Red Eagle Campground, a private facility, located at the Highway 49 turnoff.

There is a small ranger station at the campground entrance where information and backcountry camping permits can be obtained. It is open daily from 8:00 A.M. to 5:00 P.M. from mid-June to Labor Day.

The small general store located at Two Medicine Lake has some grocery items, camping supplies, and lots of souvenirs for sale. There is also a snack bar that sells hot coffee and sandwiches.

Activities

The *Sinopah,* a small tour boat, makes four trips a day up 2-mile-long Two Medicine Lake. If you take the first cruise in the morning, you can spend the day hiking from the upper end of the lake to destinations such as Upper Two Medicine Lake, No Name

Lake, or Dawson Pass, then ride the last boat down the lake in the afternoon.

Rowboats, canoes, and boats with small electric motors are available if you wish to rent a boat for transport on the lake or for fishing. Of course, you may bring your own boat, but there is a 10-hp limit on the lake. When the winds blow, the lake frequently becomes too rough for boating. However, at such times it is perfect for windsurfing.

Short Hikes

Running Eagle Falls. An easy 0.6-mile round trip, with no elevation gain, leads to a falls where the water shoots out of the rock. The trail begins 1.2 miles past the Two Medicine Entrance Station.

Rockwell Falls (trip 32)

Paradise Point. This is an easy 1.2-mile round-trip stroll, with only 100 feet of elevation gain, to a scenic peninsula on Two Medicine Lake. The trail begins from the end of the Two Medicine Road. Walk past the boat house and follow the South Shore Trail past beaver ponds and through meadows for 0.2 mile to an intersection. Turn right and walk another 0.4 mile to a gravel beach at the end of the point.

Aster Falls. The destination of this 2.4-mile round-trip walk, with a 100-foot elevation gain, is a pretty waterfall. The trail begins from the end of the Two Medicine Road. Walk past the boat house, then follow the South Shore Trail. In 1.1 miles, go left and walk the final 0.1 mile to the falls.

Twin Falls. From the Upper Boat Dock, the falls is a 1.8-mile round trip with no elevation gain. Take the Two Medicine Lake cruise, then walk up the forested valley on a wide trail.

Day Hikes And Backpacks

21 Scenic Point

Round trip: 6.2 miles (9.9 km)
Elevation gain: 2262 feet (689 m)
High point: 7522 feet (2292 m)
Hiking time: 4 hours
Day hike

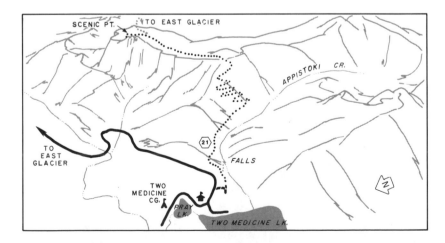

Two Medicine Lake viewed from trail to Scenic Point

Scenic Point is a misnomer; it's not just one point that is scenic, it's an entire mountain that has outstanding views over the Two Medicine area.

The trail to Scenic Point has a well-graded, continuous climb. Some sections of trail were blasted out of solid rock; other sections were etched across the loose talus slopes. To best enjoy this hike, wear sturdy shoes and carry plenty of water for the long, hot ascent.

Access: From the park entrance station on the Two Medicine Road, drive 3.3 miles up the valley. The trailhead is located on the left as the road begins its descent toward Two Medicine Lake. From the opposite direction, the trailhead is located 0.2 mile above the Two Medicine Campground entrance.

The Hike: The trail begins near the entrance of the parking area (elevation 5260 feet) and heads into the forest, climbing gradually. At 0.5 mile a side trail branches off on the right to the Appistoki Falls viewpoint.

Beyond the viewpoint, the trail begins to climb in earnest. It takes seventeen switchbacks to reach the top of Scenic Point. However, there is no need to wait for switchback 17 before you start picking out landmarks. The first views are found at the second switchback, where you can look up the Appistoki Creek basin to

Mount Henry and Appistoki Peak. To the north, Spot Mountain, Two Medicine Ridge, and the Day Fork Creek valley come into view. By the fifteenth switchback, all of Two Medicine Lake can be seen as well as Rising Wolf Mountain, Bighorn Basin, Dawson Pass, Pumpelly Pillar, Upper Two Medicine Lake, and a portion of Lower Two Medicine Lake.

At the seventeenth switchback the trail crosses a narrow saddle, then traverses a precipitous slope that should not be attempted if there is snow. Once across, the trail crosses a rocky plateau. A sign at the far end marks the point where you must head uphill to the summit of Scenic Point. There is no trail here, so stay on rocks as much as possible while crossing the fragile vegetation on the open hillside.

At the 7522-foot summit of Scenic Point, views expand to encompass the eastern plains of Montana. Below your feet are the towns of East Glacier Park and Browning, and beyond you can almost see Cut Bank, Shelby, Fargo, and New York.

The trail continues on, dropping down into the forest, to end at the outskirts of East Glacier Park.

22 Two Medicine Lake Circuit

Loop trip: 7.2 miles (11.5 km)
Elevation gain: 276 feet (84 m)
High point: 5440 feet (1658 m)
Hiking time: 4 hours
Day hike

Pack the binoculars and a substantial lunch for this hike around Two Medicine Lake. The binoculars will come in handy for spotting bighorn sheep, mountain goats, bears, and birds on the lake. The lunch needs no explanation.

The basic loop around the lake is 7.2 miles. However, you can easily add a mile or two by exploring the side trails to visit waterfalls, other lakes, or a vista point.

Access: Enter the park at Two Medicine and drive to the end of the road. Park near the store (elevation 5164 feet).

The Hike: Walk past the boat house and enter the forest, following the South Shore Trail. At 0.2 mile is an intersection and your

Sinopah Mountain (center) and Pray Lake

first opportunity to stray from the basic circuit. On the right, a trail heads 0.4 mile out to the tip of Paradise Point, where you can sit on a gravel beach and enjoy a sweeping view of the lake.

The lake trail ducks in and out of the trees for the next 0.5 mile. Shortly after you cross Aster Creek, a trail branches off on the left, designed to lure hikers off the circuit route for a 0.1-mile side trip to the base of Aster Falls and the valley overlook above.

Continue through the forest to Paradise Creek, which is crossed on a bouncy, swaying suspension bridge that is removed in the winter. At 2.4 miles, the trail to Rockwell Falls and Cobalt Lake branches off to the left. The falls, located just 1.1 nearly level miles up this trail, is another popular side trip.

Beyond the intersection, the lake trail climbs to its 5440-foot high point on a brushy slope of Sinopah Mountain where there are views of the lake, Pumpelly Pillar, and Rising Wolf Mountain.

By 3.4 miles you have passed the upper end of the lake and re-

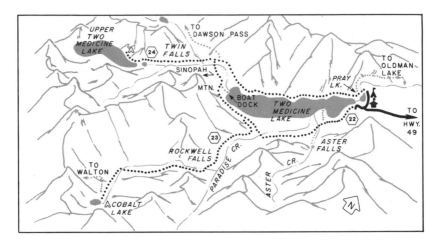

turned to the valley floor. At the intersection with the Upper Boat
Dock trail, go left and walk up-valley for a level 0.5 mile to Two
Medicine Creek and another intersection. To the left, Twin Falls is a
short 0.3-mile side trip and Upper Medicine Lake is a slightly
longer but very easy 1.7-mile trip.

The circuit route goes to the right, starting back down the lake.
At 4.1 miles is an intersection with the Dawson Pass Trail. Turn
right and walk through cool forest with occasional glimpses of the
lake. The trail passes around Pray Lake before ending in the campground. Walk to the right, through the campground, to finish the
loop back at the store.

23 Cobalt Lake

Round trip: 11.4 miles (18.2 km)
Elevation gain: 1406 feet (429 m)
High point: 6570 feet (2002 m)
Hiking time: 6 hours
Day hike or backpack

It's the colorful setting that makes this lake stand out from all
the other beautiful lakes in Glacier National Park: the rich green of
the surrounding forest and meadows, the alternating bands of
deep red and cobalt that run through the cliffs, and the bright blue
of the lake.

The hike itself ranks among the finest. This trail skirts beaver ponds, crosses several meadows, passes two waterfalls, and has several outstanding viewpoints over the Two Medicine area.

Access: At East Glacier Park, head north on Highway 49 for 4 miles. Turn left at the Two Medicine Road and drive 7.9 miles to the end of the road. **(See map on page 104.)** Park near the store (elevation 5164 feet).

The Hike: Walk past the boat dock and the boat house, then

Plank bridge on trail to Cobalt Lake

Hoary marmot

head into the forest on the South Shore Trail. After a brief climb the trail levels off and begins threading its way around beaver ponds and through grassy meadows along the base of Appistoki Peak. After just 0.2 mile the trail divides and a well-used spur goes to the right, heading out to Paradise Point. A half mile beyond, a spur trail branches left for a 0.1-mile side trip to Aster Falls.

At 2.4 miles, the Cobalt Lake Trail leaves the South Shore Trail and heads left, up Paradise Creek valley. It's a fairly level walk along the flanks of Sinopah Mountain to Cobalt Creek and Rockwell Falls at 3.5 miles. At this point you leave the valley and head up the hillside on a series of easy switchbacks.

Before long, Two Medicine Lake and the sun-dried slopes of Spot Mountain and Two Medicine Ridge come into view. The forest gives way to huckleberry fields where the berries provide hikers and bears with tasty snacks in late August.

At 5.7 miles the trail arrives at 6570-foot Cobalt Lake. The backcountry camp area is located to the left and great picnic sites are scattered all along the shore. If you have extra time and an excess of energy, continue on up to 7400-foot Two Medicine Pass, located just 2.2 miles above the lake. The pass has a commanding view over Paradise Park and the Park Creek drainage.

24 Upper Two Medicine Lake

Round trip: 9.4 miles (14.8 km)
Elevation gain: 370 feet (113 m)
High point: 5480 feet (1670 m)
Hiking time: 5 hours
Day hike or backpack

Round trip from Upper Boat Dock: 4.4 miles (7 km)
Elevation gain: 320 feet (98 m)
High point: 5480 feet (1670 m)
Hiking time: 2½ hours
Day hike or backpack

The hike to Upper Two Medicine Lake offers an excellent opportunity for family groups of all ages and energy levels to enjoy a taste of the backcountry. Day hikers will experience a cool forest walk with a side trip to Twin Falls. At the upper lake there is a place to splash young feet and a tremendous view for the older and more reflective minds. Overnight hikers will have the extra pleasure of watching the brook trout jumping for their dinner and counting a million stars after sunset.

For little feet, and many older ones, a ride on the tour boat will add immeasurable pleasure to the hike, as well as reduce the distance the packs must be carried. The tour boat, called the *Sinopah*,

Upper boat dock on Two Medicine Lake

takes about 30 minutes to reach the Upper Boat Dock.

Access: Hikers planning to walk the entire distance will find the trail by driving through the Two Medicine Campground to the hikers' parking area at the outlet of Pray Lake (elevation 5170 feet). If you plan to ride the tour boat up the lake, drive to the end of the road and park near the boat dock. Tickets are purchased at the boat.

The Hike: Cross Two Medicine Creek on a wide bridge and walk 100 feet to a junction. Go left on the North Shore Trail.

After winding through the forest for 3 miles, the trail divides; the Dawson Pass Trail to No Name Lake takes off to the right, Upper Two Medicine Lake is to the left. Just 0.1 mile farther is a second junction, this one with the trail from the Upper Boat Dock. Stay to the right and walk 0.2 mile to a third junction, with the trail to Twin Falls, a short and easy side trip.

The trail continues through forest interspersed with occasional fields of huckleberries. Make plenty of noise and watch for bears in the late summer.

At 4.7 miles the trail arrives at Upper Two Medicine Lake. Pumpelly Pillar and Mount Helen soar above the north shore. On the south side the rocky slopes of Rising Bull Ridge climb high above the emerald waters, and at the upper end of the lake Lone Walker Mountain dominates the skyline.

25 Dawson Pass Loop

Loop hike: 15.4 miles (24.6 km)
Elevation gain: 2916 feet (889 m)
High point: 8080 feet (2463 m)
Hiking time: 2–3 days
Backpack

Enjoy an eagle's-eye view of four valleys from one of the most scenic stretches of high alpine trail in Glacier National Park. This loop is a must for all backpackers.

The loop begins and ends at the Two Medicine Campground. The optimum itinerary for the hike would be to walk to Oldman Lake the first night, then either complete the loop the following day or spend the second night at No Name Lake or Upper Two Medicine Lake. This schedule allows hikers to make the best use of the ter-

Fossilized algae form distinctive patterns in sandstone found near Dawson Pass

rain and trails. However, this is a popular loop and it is often difficult to get a backcountry camping permit. Be flexible with your itinerary; this trip is worth it.

Access: From the park entrance station on Lower Two Medicine Lake, drive 4.5 miles to the Two Medicine Lake Campground. Go right, passing a small ranger's office, and drive through the camp area to find the hikers' parking area at the lower end of Pray Lake (elevation 5163 feet).

The Hike: To begin the loop, walk across the Two Medicine Creek Bridge and on for 100 feet to an intersection. Go right on a trail that contours around the flanks of Rising Wolf Mountain, then descends into Dry Fork Valley. At 1.8 miles cross the aptly named Dry Fork Creek, then go left and continue up the valley.

At 5 miles the trail divides. Oldman Lake and camp area are located 0.5 mile to the left (elevation 6640 feet). Note that the forest floor near the camp area has a thick covering of huckleberries; watch for bears in the late summer.

From Oldman Lake it is only 1.6 miles and a few steep switchbacks to the 7580-foot summit of Pitamakan Pass. The climb continues above the pass as the trail traverses open slopes, passing intersections with the trail to Morning Star Lake and the Cut Bank Ranger Station and the trail to Cut Bank Pass and Nyack Creek. After gaining 500 feet in 0.7 mile, you reach the 8080-foot trip high point: the Pitamakan Pass Overlook.

The overlook marks the start of an incredibly scenic section of alpine trail that contours around Mount Morgan to a narrow pass, then traverses the side of Flinsch Peak to a rocky shoulder over-looking Dawson Pass.

The trail descends on excellently graded switchbacks for 400 feet to 7598-foot Dawson Pass, then plummets down the rocky hill-side for 1.2 miles to the No Name Lake intersection. Continuing

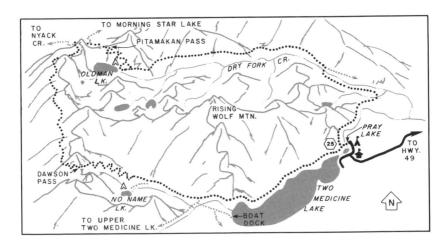

Hiker overlooking Oldman Lake

down, the rate of descent slackens for the final mile to the upper end of Two Medicine Lake.

To complete the loop, walk the forested North Shore Trail for a final 3.1 miles along Two Medicine Lake to the campground. Or, walk over to the Upper Boat Dock and let the *Sinopah* carry you and your pack for 2 miles down the lake.

26 Firebrand Pass

Round trip: 9.4 miles (14.8 km)
Elevation gain: 1867 feet (569 m)
High point: 6951 feet (2119 m)
Hiking time: 5 hours
Day hike

During the fire of 1910, a burning ember blew from the west, over the pass, to set the east side ablaze. Since that time, the name Firebrand has stuck to this pass.

The forest has been slow to return to the high alpine country around Firebrand Pass, and the views are unobstructed except by sturdy old tree trunks bleached white by time, ghosts of the old forest.

The Firebrand Pass Trail lies in the southeast section of Glacier National Park. This is a relatively pristine area, having escaped the mobs that flock to other parts of the park. The views in this area are fascinating. Looking east one can see the foothills of the Rocky Mountains sloping down to a vast prairie that extends far beyond the visible horizon. In the fall this is an excellent location to look for elk or to listen to the bulls try out the strength of their bugling calls.

Access: Drive Highway 2 east from Marias Pass for 5.2 miles or west from East Glacier Park for 6.4 miles. The unsigned turnoff is on the northwest side of the highway. There are two dirt access roads, so if you miss the first you can catch the second. The road descends and crosses the railroad tracks; the trailhead is 20 feet beyond the track (elevation 5084 feet).

The Hike: Use the hikers' access to pass through the fence that marks the national park boundary, then follow an old road around a couple of beaver ponds. At 0.2 mile the trail takes off on the left, crossing a grassy field, then heading up the forested hillside, paralleling Coonsa Creek.

The first of two intersections is reached at 1.7 miles. Go right on Autumn Creek Trail and traverse along the base of the mountains. Watch for prints, trails, and other signs of elk in the meadows and along the creeks in this area.

The second intersection is reached at 2.2 miles (elevation 5540

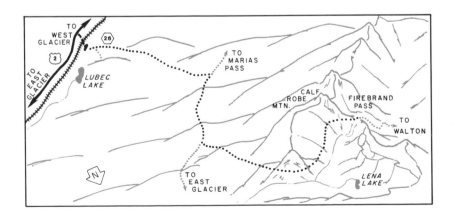

Hiker on trail to Firebrand Pass

feet). Go left on the Firebrand Trail and begin the climb to the pass. At the end of the first climb, your breath will be coming in gasps. Not to worry; the trail soon settles into a steady, comfortable ascent. Contour around Calf Robe Mountain, then enter a subalpine basin at the base of the pass.

The trail climbs, traversing the talus slopes, to reach the wind-swept summit of 6951-foot Firebrand Pass at 4.7 miles. This is wide-open country with opportunities for roaming. With a good map it is a relatively easy cross-country trip to Lena Lake, or the summit of Red Crow Mountain, or over the shoulder of Calf Robe Mountain to find the trail on the other side.

CUT BANK

The North Fork Cut Bank Creek valley is located on the east side of the park between Two Medicine and St. Mary. Mother Nature has done a beautiful job of landscaping this valley, painting the dry hills in brilliant yellows, outlining rocky mountain summits with bold strokes against the deep blue sky, and setting the creek on a meandering path through the forest and the wide, grassy meadows.

Accommodations And Services

Cut Bank is accessed by a 5-mile-long dirt road with no services at the end except a small campground. Most people who use this area come to hike in the backcountry for overnight or extended trips. The day hikes out of Cut Bank are all long, with round-trip mileages of more than 10 miles.

There is a ranger in residence at Cut Bank who can be contacted in case of an emergency. Backcountry hiking permits are not issued here.

The campground has nineteen sites, pit toilets, and running water. Trailers and large units are not recommended.

Mountain goat

Upper basin of Hudson Bay Creek from Triple Divide Pass

Day Hikes And Backpacks

27 Triple Divide Pass

Round trip: 14 miles (22.4 km)
Elevation gain: 2227 feet (679 m)
High point: 7397 feet (2254 m)
Hiking time: 7 hours
Day hike or backpack

Triple Divide Pass is as close as you can get by trail to Triple Divide Peak, one of the most unusual points on the North American continent. Triple Divide is a triangular peak that serves as the meeting point for three major watersheds. A drop of water on the summit of Triple Divide Peak could roll west, down the Pacific Creek drainage, to find its way to the Columbia River and on to the Pacific Ocean. Or, a gust of wind might push that droplet north, where it would descend to the St. Mary River and end up in Hudson

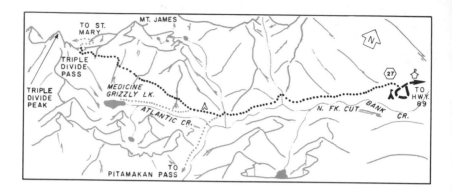

Bay. Or, a mountain goat might come along and step on the droplet and send it down the Atlantic Creek drainage to the Missouri River and the Gulf of Mexico.

Most hikers would love to stand on the summit of Triple Divide Peak and empty a water bottle just to watch the water start its journey to three different oceans. However, steep rock walls and junky rock preclude all but skilled climbers with ropes and hard hats from ascending the peak. Hikers must be satisfied with Triple Divide Pass and finding a point where water will flow equally toward the Atlantic Ocean and Hudson Bay.

The hike to the divide may be accomplished in a long day or as a backpack with a base camp at Atlantic Creek.

Access: Drive Highway 89 south for 15 miles from St. Mary, then head west on the dirt-surfaced Cut Bank Road for 5 miles to the trailhead (elevation 5170 feet).

The Hike: The trail heads up the valley, paralleling the North Fork Cut Bank Creek while passing through forest interspersed with grassy meadows. When the first intersection is reached at 3.9 miles, only 160 feet of elevation have been gained.

At the intersection, the trail divides. The Pitamakan Pass Trail goes left, climbing to Morning Star Lake and Pitamakan Pass. The Triple Divide Trail follows the right fork and heads up the Atlantic Creek valley. After 0.4 mile the trail passes the forested Atlantic Creek backcountry camp area. There are four tent spaces here, and campfires are allowed.

Just 0.2 mile above the camp area, the trail to Medicine Grizzly Lake branches off on the left, heading up the valley for another, nearly level 1.2 miles to the lakeshore. Triple Divide Pass Trail goes to the right.

The final 2.6 miles to the pass are spent in a long ascending traverse. The trail grade never seems to vary as it heads straight across the hillside over talus slopes and through the rocky ribs of Mount James. Watch for mountain sheep on the ledges above the trail. Rocks tumbling down the hillside are frequently a sign that there are sheep above, even if you can't see them.

Triple Divide Pass (elevation 7397 feet) is reached 7.1 miles from the Cut Bank trailhead. The pass is surrounded by mountains: Norris, Split, Triple Divide, Razoredge, Medicine Grizzly, and James, to name just a few.

Bicycling

28 Cut Bank

Round trip: 10 miles (16 km)
Elevation gain: 100 feet (30 m)
High point: 5200 feet (1585 m)
Riding time: 2 hours
Surface: dirt road
Difficulty: easy

Simplicity is the word that best describes this short ride to Cut Bank. The scene is one of simple pastoral elegance, with cattle grazing on the open grasslands along the banks of North Cut Bank Creek. The road is well graded and lightly traveled, making for ex-

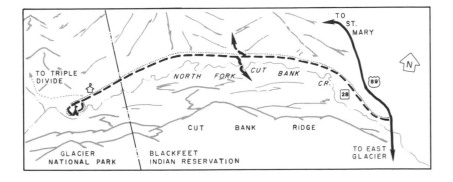

Open meadows in North Fork Cut Bank Creek valley

cellent riding. This portion of the Cut Bank valley is nearly level, and the miles fly by. Even the directions for the trip are not difficult to follow, as there are no turns to worry about. The ride ends at the Cut Bank Campground, a nice place for a picnic and a short stroll along the creek before heading back. Sounds very simple, doesn't it?

Access: From the town of St. Mary, drive south on Highway 89 for 15 miles to the Cut Bank turnoff. There is no specific parking area here, so find a place along the edge of the road.

Log:

0.0 mile   Dab a little insect repellent on any exposed skin, ride your bike across the cattle guard, and head up-valley on a nearly smooth, gravel-surfaced road. The road crosses Blackfeet Indian land, so please curb any urges you might have to stop and explore. The scenery is excellent.

Ahead, the horizon is a wall of mountains with marvelous names such as Mad Wolf, Bad Marriage, White Calf, and Kupunkamint.

2.3 miles Pass a spur road on the right, followed by one on the left. Continue straight over the open meadows, watching for deer, birds, and, of course, cow patties on the road.

4.1 miles A cattle guard marks the entrance to the national park.

4.6 miles Pass the Cut Bank Ranger Station on the right.

5.0 miles A parking area, usually full to overflowing, marks the Cut Bank trailhead.

5.1 miles Reach the Cut Bank Campground, with picnic tables, water, and pit toilets. This is a great place for a lunch stop before heading back. Deer are often seen roaming the campground, looking for scraps left on tables, so make sure your area is clean when you leave.

Mule deer

ST. MARY

St. Mary is more than just a place at the eastern end of the Going-to-the-Sun Road, it is an area that encompasses all the geographical features that bear the St. Mary name. And the list of St. Marys is impressive. It includes a waterfall, a river, two lakes—one 10 miles long and the other 6 miles long—a glacier-carved valley, a campground, a visitor center, a town, and innumerable scenic viewpoints and stunning vistas.

Accommodations And Services

The town of St. Mary lies outside of the park boundary, and the motels there and the St. Mary Lodge are private enterprises. The Rising Sun Motor Inn, located 6 miles west of town on the Going-to-the-Sun Road, is inside the park and run by Glacier Park, Inc. Guests at the Rising Sun Motor Inn can buy meals at the coffee shop and snack bar or drive to St. Mary and eat at one of the town's informal eateries.

Fishing at St. Mary River

St. Mary Lake from Sun Point

The park has two campgrounds in the vicinity of St. Mary Lake: Rising Sun Campground, which has 83 sites, and St. Mary Campground, which has 156 sites. Evening campfire programs are a feature of the Rising Sun area. Guests at St. Mary Campground walk to the visitor center for a nightly slide show. In July and August Rising Sun Campground is full by noon; St. Mary Campground is usually full by dinnertime. Outside of the park, there are four privately operated campgrounds in the town of St. Mary and along the shores of Lower St. Mary Lake.

Groceries and an endless variety of T-shirts can be purchased at the Rising Sun camp store. A more complete selection of souvenirs is available in town. The St. Mary grocery store has a sporting goods shop and the town post office on the premises. The town also has two gas stations.

Showers are available through the Rising Sun Motor Inn, and tokens are purchased at the camp store. There is a small laundromat in St. Mary, located in an unmarked building across from the lodge. Be sure to bring your own change and detergent.

Activities

The St. Mary Visitor Center is always a busy place. There are exhibits, an auditorium where a Glacier National Park slide program is shown throughout the day, a small store where books and maps may be purchased, an information desk staffed by a park naturalist, and a special desk for issuing backcountry use permits.

A scenic cruise on St. Mary Lake is a popular way to see the area's spectacular scenery. The boat dock is located just west of the Rising Sun area, and the cruise lasts for an hour and a half with an optional 15-minute walk to Baring Falls. Some cruises can be combined with a 2-hour walk to St. Mary Falls with a park naturalist.

The 1913 Ranger Station is an interesting place to visit. It is located at the Red Eagle Lake trailhead (see trip 29). The old ranger station has been refurbished and is now a museum of life in the park in the early 1900s. The buildings are opened to the public on special occasions, but most of the time visitors must be satisfied with peering in the windows.

Short Hikes

Sun Point. This 1-mile loop trip on a self-guided nature trail begins at the Sun Point picnic area, 9 miles west of St. Mary. Walk

St. Mary Falls

out to the point for a view of the lake, then follow the lakeshore trail to the former site of the Going-to-the-Sun Chalet.

St. Mary Falls. A 1.6-mile round trip takes you to a beautiful falls. Drive the Going-to-the-Sun Road 10.9 miles west of the St. Mary Entrance Station and park on the left side of the road.

Sunrift Gorge. This 200-foot round-trip walk is a steep climb to a fascinating gorge. Baring Creek has cut deeply into a fault fracture, and the resulting narrow passageway is a favorite with photographers. The gorge is located 10.4 miles west of the St. Mary Entrance Station on the Going-to-the-Sun Road. You may also walk down for 0.3 mile from the gorge to Baring Falls.

Day Hikes And Backpacks

29 Red Eagle Lake

Round trip: 15.4 miles (24.6 km)
Elevation gain: 300 feet (91 m)
High point: 4840 feet (1475 m)
Hiking time: 7 hours
Day hike or backpack

The miles of grassy meadows, which provide habitat for herds of elk, deer, and an occasional mountain lion, make this a unique hike in Glacier National Park.

Red Eagle Lake is a popular destination with day hikers, who come to enjoy the scenery of this glacier-carved valley; with backpackers, who pause there on the popular 23.2-mile traverse be-

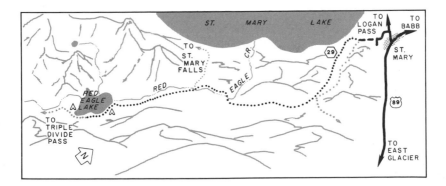

Trail through open meadows on way to Red Eagle Lake

tween St. Mary and Cut Bank; and with fishermen, who throng to this lake, carrying inflatable rafts on their backs, to try their luck with the feisty cutthroats.

(Note: The bridges are dismantled in the winter. If you plan to hike here in early summer or after the middle of September, check with a ranger before starting out.)

Access: From the Highway 89 turnoff at the town of St. Mary, drive 0.3 mile toward the park entrance. Turn left and follow the signs to the trailhead (elevation 4540 feet).

The Hike: There are two ways to begin the hike. The standard method is to follow the Red Eagle Lake Trail along an abandoned road that climbs from the shores of St. Mary Lake to a grassy plateau. The alternative method is to start the trip by following a less-used trail that begins directly behind the 1913 Ranger Station and climbs through forest to join the main trail at 1.2 miles.

At 3.8 miles the road ends and a trail continues on, dropping down a steep bank into the Red Eagle Creek valley. Once the creek is crossed on a suspension bridge, the trail heads up-valley, traversing meadows and forest. A mile later the trail divides. Follow the left fork, which recrosses Red Eagle Creek on a second suspension bridge.

The final 2.9 miles pass quickly as the trail continues to traverse alternating bands of trees and meadows. Red Eagle Lake (elevation 4722 feet) is reached at 7.7 miles. The backpackers' campsite straddles the trail near the edge of the lake. There is a second camp area, located at the upper end of the lake, that is designed for horsepacker and backpacker use. Day hikers will find a gravel beach and rock outcroppings at the lower end of the lake, perfect for picnicking and sunbathing.

30 Otokomi Lake

Round trip: 10 miles (16 km)
Elevation gain: 1900 feet (579 m)
High point: 6660 feet (2030 m)
Hiking time: 6 hours
Day hike or backpack

The most lasting impression of Otokomi Lake is one of intense color. The lake is located in Rose Basin, and the rock walls surrounding the lake are a deep, dark, throbbing red. Add to this the

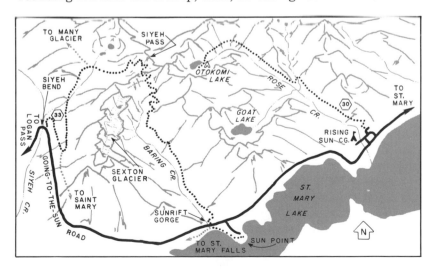

Otokomi Lake

bright green highlights of the stunted alpine firs and meadow grass, snow in blinding patches of white, and an intensely blue sky. The result is an amazingly colorful scene.

Access: Drive the Going-to-the-Sun Road 7.5 miles west from the town of St. Mary to the Rising Sun Resort and Campground. Park at the General Store (elevation 4560 feet).

The Hike: Following the "TRAIL" sign, walk the paved road uphill, past the motel units. At the first intersection, stay left; at the second, go right to find the trailhead at the next corner.

After a mile spent climbing a forested hillside, the trail emerges from the trees to skim along the precipitous edge of the impressive Rose Creek Gorge. The gorge is paralleled until it ends at a large waterfall.

Beyond the gorge, the trail parallels the creek as it plunges through a series of intriguing cascades. At about 4 miles there is a sudden descent into a subalpine valley where meadows and huckleberry fields alternate with stands of trees. The trail loses its well-graded quality, and the climbs become steep and abrupt. The head of the valley comes into view, but the lake remains hidden.

At 5 miles the trail drops to a three-site backcountry campground. Day hikers should descend to the creek, then go right to the lakeshore. A boot-beaten path heads around the lake in both directions, allowing hikers to find their own personal picnic sites and rock-skipping areas along the shore.

31 The Falls Hike

Round trip: 6 miles (9.6 km)
Elevation gain: 300 feet (91 m)
High point: 4800 feet (1463 m)
Hiking time: 3 hours
Day hike

This forested hike to three waterfalls is a great way to spend a warm afternoon. Bathe your feet in a creek, cool your face in the

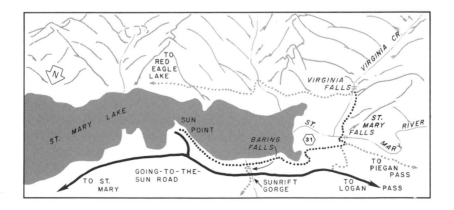

Virginia Falls

spray, or just sit in the shade and let the water and the world rush by.

Access: The hike has two access points. The true start is from Sun Point, located 9.6 miles west of the St. Mary Entrance Station on the Going-to-the-Sun Road. The second is a short-cut access that begins at a small turnout 10.9 miles west of the St. Mary entrance. This access bypasses Baring Falls.

The Hike: From Sun Point, the hike starts out following the nature trail along the shore of St. Mary Lake. Take time to walk out on the point, where a location-finder sign names all the major peaks. The trail heads up the lake, passing the site of the old Going-to-the-Sun chalets, then passes over the low cliffs that line the rocky shore.

At 0.7 miles the trail divides. The right fork heads up to Sunrift

Gorge in 0.3 mile. If you haven't explored the deep, narrow channel cut by Baring Creek, this is a highly recommended side trip.

A few feet beyond the intersection is Baring Falls, the least spectacular and most accessible of the three falls. Beyond the falls, the trail returns briefly to the lakeshore and the site of the tour boat dock, then heads back into the shade of a thick lodgepole forest.

At 1.7 miles the short-cut access trail from the Going-to-the-Sun Road joins on the right. A few feet beyond is another intersection; stay left. The thundering roar of water signals your arrival at St. Mary Falls, 2.5 miles from Sun Point. Here the St. Mary River is crossed on a wide bridge, and hikers may linger in the refreshing mist.

The trail continues to wind through the forest, climbing steadily along cascading Virginia Creek for the final 0.5 mile to Virginia Falls. The falls is visible from the trail; however, if you want to bathe your feet in the clear pool at its base, scramble up the rough path along the right-hand side of the creek. An outhouse is located on the main trail, across the footbridge.

32 Gunsight Lake

Round trip: 12.6 miles (20.2 km)
Elevation gain: 1040 feet in (317 m); 640 feet out (195 m)
High point: 5680 feet (1731 m)
Hiking time: 6 hours
Day hike or backpack

One way to Lake McDonald: 19.8 miles (32 km)
Elevation gain: 3966 feet (1209 m)
High point: 7360 feet (2243 m)
Hiking time: 2–3 days
Backpack

Gunsight Lake is not only a popular day hike, it is also part of the well-known traverse between St. Mary Lake and Lake McDonald. Hikers making the traverse can leave their cars at the Lake McDonald Lodge, ride the shuttle bus to the trailhead, and still have plenty of time to reach the first night's camp at Gunsight Lake.

Access: The hike begins at the scenic Jackson Glacier turnout (elevation 5280 feet) on the Going-to-the-Sun Road, 13.2 miles west of the St. Mary Entrance Station or 4.9 miles east of Logan Pass.

The Hike: The hike begins with a heartbreaking descent in which 640 feet of elevation are lost in 1.5 miles. The descent ends when the trail reaches Deadwood Falls and the intersection with the St. Mary Lake Trail.

From the intersection, go straight across Reynolds Creek, passing a small campsite reserved for Continental Divide Trail hikers, then heading up the St. Mary River valley. The base of the valley is wide and swampy, ideal habitat for deer and elk, and the climb is very gradual.

At 4.3 miles a spur trail to Florence Falls branches off on the right. Shortly beyond this intersection, you leave the forest and begin a traverse across the brushy flanks of Fusillade Mountain. Views of glaciers and mountains (Citadel, Logan, Blackfoot, and Jackson) fill the horizon. Below, Siksika Falls glistens brightly in the dark forest. At 6.2 miles there is a gradual descent, which ends

Gunsight Lake with Gunsight Pass in distance

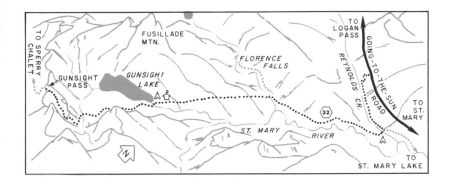

in 0.1 mile at the lakeshore and a backcountry campsite (elevation 5680 feet).

Hikers continuing on to Lake McDonald must cross the outlet of Gunsight Lake and follow the trail over the high alpine tundra for another 2.8 miles to 6946-foot Gunsight Pass. (Note: The bridge over the outlet stream is removed in September; check with the ranger before starting out.) Hikers who linger at the pass may find themselves the center of attention from squirrels looking for handouts and mountain goats looking for salt.

From the pass it is 4.4 miles to Glacier Basin, where the Sperry Campground and Sperry Chalet are located. The final 6.4 miles of the traverse are a forested descent to Lake McDonald (see trip 3 for details).

33 Siyeh Pass

Round trip: 9.4 miles (15 km)
Elevation gain: 2390 feet (723 m)
High point: 8240 feet (2512 m)
Hiking time: 6 hours
Day hike

Meadows, lakes, and alpine views are the main attractions of this hike through some of the highest country traversed by trail in Glacier National Park.

Siyeh Pass may be hiked as a round trip from the parking lot at Siyeh Bend or as a one-way excursion from Siyeh Bend to Sunrift

Preston Park (center) with Piegan Mountain (right), Heavy Runner and Reynolds mountains (left)

Gorge. The one-way option is 10.3 miles (16.5 km) long and you must arrange your own transportation back to the trailhead or walk another mile along St. Mary Lake to catch the shuttle bus at Sun Point.

Access: Drive or ride the shuttle bus to Siyeh Bend, located 15.6 miles west of the town of St. Mary on the Going-to-the-Sun Road. (From the opposite direction, Siyeh Bend is located 3 miles east of Logan Pass.) The hike begins at 5850 feet, across the road from the parking area. **(See map on page 125.)**

The Hike: Follow the Siyeh Bend Cutoff Trail along Siyeh Creek, then head uphill into the forest. At 1.5 miles (elevation 6260 feet), the Cutoff Trail ends. Go left on the Piegan Pass Trail and head north through alternating bands of meadows and trees. This is grizzly habitat, so watch for tracks and scat and make plenty noise whether you see any sign or not.

At 2.8 miles the trail divides; the left fork continues on to Many Glacier. Go right and head into Preston Park, a beautiful subalpine area of small lakes and open meadows. Take time to wander around one of these ponds to catch a view of Piegan, Heavy Runner, and Reynolds mountains reflected in the shallow waters.

At the upper end of Preston Park, leave the meadows and switchback up the rocky talus slopes. The trail reaches 7750-foot Siyeh Pass and continues to climb barren slopes until it reaches 8240 feet, where it levels off for a short distance over a barren talus slope. A 100-foot descent to an unnamed, wind-blasted col marks the turnaround point for hikers heading back to Siyeh Bend.

If you opt to continue down to Sunrift Gorge, there is a long, well-graded descent through open meadows to look forward to. At 0.6 mile below the col, an abandoned trail branches right to Sexton Glacier.

As the descent continues, waterfalls come into view, streaming off the cliffs below the glacier. Eventually these streams flow together and hurtle down the bright red bedrock and into Sunrift Gorge at the Going-to-the-Sun Road.

Any hikers who plan to catch the shuttle at Sun Point must follow the gorge trail under the road and descend for 0.3 mile to the lakeshore. Go left at the intersection and walk along the lakeshore for 0.7 mile to Sun Point.

Bicycling

34 St. Mary to Waterton Park

One way: 48.3 miles (77.3 km)
Elevation gain: 1700 feet (518 m)
High point: 5520 feet (1683 m)
Riding time: 7 hours
Surface: paved road
Difficulty: moderate

There aren't too many places in the world where you can go through four nations in less than 50 miles. However, on the ride from St. Mary to the Waterton townsite, cyclists pass over lands owned by four different nations: the United States, the Blackfeet Indian Nation, Canada, and the Blood Indians.

To truly explore this fascinating and scenic area, it is best to pack the touring bags and spend a day or more in Waterton Lakes before returning to Glacier. However, riders with a need for speed should have no trouble riding to Waterton and back in a single day.

(Note: This ride crosses the international border at Chief Mountain. The border crossing is only open from mid-May to mid-September.)

Chief Mountain International Highway

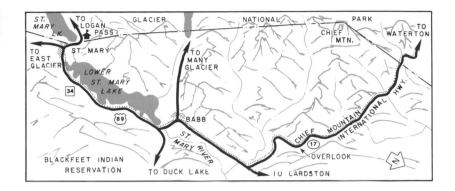

Access: Drive to the town of St. Mary at the eastern end of the Going-to-the-Sun Road. Park near the St. Mary Lodge (elevation 4541 feet).

Log:

0.0 mile   Head north through the town of St. Mary on Highway 89. This road has a rough, narrow shoulder in town and a wider shoulder in the open country. The terrain is rolling as the road heads around Lower St. Mary Lake. Most of this portion of the ride is through Blackfeet Indian land.

6.2 miles   Pass a KOA campground on the left, notable for its name, Chewing Black Bones. The camp was named in honor of a Blackfeet elder, born in 1859.

7.5 miles   Highway 464 branches off on the right. Continue straight on Highway 89, crossing the St. Mary River. Notice the direction of the water flow. Like all rivers in this area, the St. Mary is on its way to Hudson Bay.

8.6 miles   Enter the town of Babb—just large enough to have a post office, a general store, a couple of bars, and a motel.

8.7 miles   The road to Many Glacier branches off to the left.

13.2 miles   Turn left onto Highway 17, also known as the Chief Mountain International Highway. There is a small store at this junction, the last chance to buy food for 35.1 miles. Highway 17 begins by climbing enthusiastically out of the valley to the crest of the foothills and to views.

18.2 miles   The climb ends at the Crusher Hill Scenic Overlook (elevation 5500 feet), a great place to stop and enjoy the view. Chief Mountain dominates the western horizon.

To the east, the prairie spreads out for miles. From this point on, the highway heads over rolling hills. Watch for cattle on the road.

24.2 miles A cattle guard marks the entrance to Glacier National Park, and the aspen forest gives way to lodgepole forest.

26.9 miles Start a 3.5-mile descent.

27.6 miles Pass the Belly River trailhead on the left. Just ahead is the Chief Mountain border crossing. Ride past the U.S. Customs without stopping.

27.8 miles Canadian Customs: stop here to show identification. If you look a bit scruffy they may also ask you to prove that you have some source of monetary funding for your stay in Canada. Across the border the road continues downhill with a wide shoulder.

30.4 miles Pass the turnoff to the Belly River Campground on the left. The road levels as it crosses the Belly River valley.

30.8 miles An exhibit on the left explains the 4050-acre Blood Indian Forest Reserve.

31.7 miles Cross the Belly River and enter the Blood Indian Forest Reserve. Before long the road begins a steep climb out of the valley.

34.8 miles End of climb. The road now reenters Waterton Lakes National Park, then heads across a high plateau covered with beaver ponds and aspens.

35.3 miles Pass a small picnic area on the right.

36.3 miles The Lewis Overthrust Exhibit. You don't have to be a geologist to be interested in how a 600-million-year-old mountain ended up on top of 100-million-year-old bedrock.

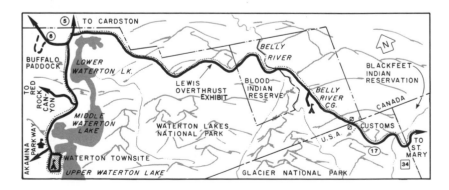

Belly River

37.8 miles Viewpoint over the Waterton Lakes. A mountain finder helps you name all the visible landmarks. The road begins a 2-mile descent. The speed limit is 80 km per hour (50 mph), so watch that speedometer.

41.9 miles Reach a junction; go left on Highway 5 West.

42.3 miles The Maskinonge Picnic Area is on the left. This is a typical example of a picnic area in Waterton Lakes National Park. In addition to rest rooms, running water, and picnic tables, there are cooking shelters, wood stoves, and a pile of split wood ready for burning.

42.4 miles   Cross the Waterton River bridge, then turn left toward the Waterton townsite. (Just 0.3 mile ahead on the main road is a buffalo paddock. An overlook provides a chance to view buffalo in the semi-wild.)

42.7 miles   At the wildlife viewing area on the right is an osprey nest on an abandoned powerline pole.

43 miles   Entrance station to Waterton Lakes National Park. Park use fees are collected here.

43.5 miles   Pass the Knights Lake Picnic Area turnoff on the left. The shoulder narrows, then disappears as the road climbs above Lower Waterton Lake.

44.5 miles   Kootenai Brown's gravesite is accessed by a trail on the left. Brown was the first park warden at Waterton Lakes.

45.8 miles   The Red Rock Canyon Parkway branches off on the right. If you plan on staying several days in the park, the ride up the Blakiston Creek valley to the canyon is a must.

45.9 miles   Cross Blakiston Creek and then pedal by the Pass Creek Picnic Area.

46.3 miles   A turnoff to the golf course is on the right; the stables and the Markes Hole Picnic Area are to the left.

47 miles   Pass a small picnic area on the left; tables only, no water.

47.3 miles   A boat launch and the Linnet Lake Nature Trail are on the left.

47.7 miles   On the left is the entrance to the Prince of Wales Hotel; on the right are the Information Centre and the Bears Hump trailhead. At the Information Centre you can find out about lodging or camping as well as boat tours, hikes, rides, and exchanging money.

47.9 miles   The Akamina Parkway junction is on the right and a picnic area is on the left.

48.1 miles   Enter the town of Waterton Park. Take the first left to find the stores, restaurants, and motels. There is a bike shop in the Tamarack Mall if you need any replacement parts.

48.3 miles   To reach the campground, take a right at the tour boat parking lot entrance.

LOGAN PASS

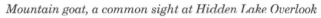

At 6680 feet, Logan Pass is the highest point on the Going-to-the-Sun Road, and for many people it is the high point of a visit to Glacier National Park. The pass lies at timberline and has an ideal mixture of subalpine and alpine environments: dwarfed trees and verdant meadows. Beautiful fields of flowers lure visitors away from their cars for long walks along the Garden Wall or through the Hanging Gardens. Mountains provide dramatic backdrops for family portraits. Wildlife watching fascinates young and old. Visitors arrive planning to spend an hour at the pass and end up spending all day.

Because Logan Pass is the scenic highlight of the park, it is crowded. From midmorning to late afternoon, finding parking at the summit is difficult to impossible. To avoid problems, try to arrive before 10:00 A.M. or after 4:00 P.M.

Logan Pass has a very fragile environment, and the meadows take years to regrow if they are trampled. When walking through

Mountain goat, a common sight at Hidden Lake Overlook

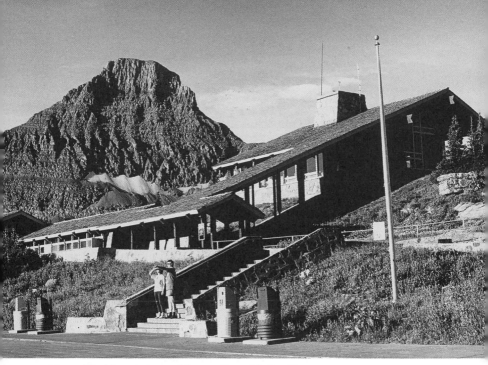

Reynolds Mountain and Logan Pass Visitor Center

the alpine flower fields, stay on the established trail. Do not pick the flowers. Do not feed the animals.

Weather can be a major factor at the pass. In the high alpine environment there is no shelter from the wind and rain. It may even snow in July or August. You never can predict mountain weather, so bring warm clothing and sunscreen on every walk.

Services

The visitor center is the best place to have your questions answered concerning places to walk to and types of flowers you will see. The center has a bookstore, exhibits on the alpine environment, rest rooms, and running water.

No food service, lodging, or gas is available at Logan Pass.

Activities

Wildlife viewing is one of the favorite activities at Logan Pass. Squirrels, hoary marmots, ptarmigan, deer, mountain goats, mountain sheep, and bears are frequently sighted from the parking area. Mountain goats are nearly always seen on the rocks above the trail at the Hidden Lake Overlook.

Rangers lead daily hikes along the Garden Wall or to the Hidden Lake Overlook. Naturalists talk about the alpine environment during short guided walks in the vicinity of the visitor center.

Short Hikes

Hidden Lake Nature Trail. This nature trail is a 1.5-mile round-trip tour through the alpine meadows, with an elevation gain of 400 feet. The trail begins above the visitor center, then heads up over the meadows on a boardwalk. The trail continues on to Hidden Lake. The National Park Service asks that hikers stay on the trail in this area to protect the fragile alpine meadows. Do not venture off the boardwalk or trail.

Day Hikes And Backpacks

35 Hidden Lake

Round trip to Hidden Lake Overlook: 3 miles (5 km)
Elevation gain: 480 feet (146 m)
High point: 7130 feet (2173 m)
Hiking time: 1½ hours
Day hike

Round trip to Hidden Lake: 6 miles (9.6 km)
Elevation gain: 480 feet in (146 m); 755 feet out (230 m)
High point: 7130 feet (2173 m)
Hiking time: 4 hours
Day hike

No visit to Glacier National Park is complete without a hike on the Hidden Lake Trail. This short trail allows hikers to explore the elements that are the very essence of the park: the flower-laden meadows, the glaciers, the jagged peaks that form the Garden Wall, the wildlife, and a lake carved by ancient glaciers. It is not necessary to walk the entire distance to get the feel of the area. The meadows begin at the trailhead, and so do the views. At a bare minimum, plan to walk the nature loop, which is located at the trailhead.

Access: Drive the Going-to-the-Sun Road to Logan Pass and park at the summit (elevation 6375 feet).

Hanging Gardens (left) and Reynolds Mountain

The Hike: Start your hike by following the paved pathway up the hill next to the visitor center.

The Hidden Lake Trail heads out over the meadows. As a result of the trail's popularity and the fragile nature of the meadows it crosses, an intricate boardwalk has been built to keep feet off the delicate hillside. Hikers are requested to stay on the boardwalk as it climbs over the flower-covered terraces of the Hanging Gardens. Once in the meadows, watch for ground squirrels, hoary marmots, and ptarmigan.

The boardwalk ends at the base of Clements Mountain by the edge of an old moraine. The glacier has receded to a patch of dirty ice; however, the moraine remains in excellent shape, outlining the former boundaries of the ice.

A wide path continues on from the boardwalk, passing several streams and a couple of flower-festooned waterfalls. At 1.2 miles the trail enters Hidden Lake Pass. Turn your binoculars on the lower slopes of Clements Mountain and search for mountain goats, which spend their mornings sunbathing on the ledges above the trail.

At the far end of the pass is the Hidden Lake Overlook. This is the ideal turnaround point for most hikers. From the viewing platform, it is possible to look down on the large lake, 755 feet below, boxed in by Bearhat Mountain to the west, glacier-covered Gunsight Mountain to the south, and Cannon and Clements mountains to the north.

For those who decide to continue on, the next 1.5 miles down to Hidden Lake are rough. The trail weaves its way through bands of cliffs with some steep sections. Wear sturdy shoes and don't forget your fishing pole.

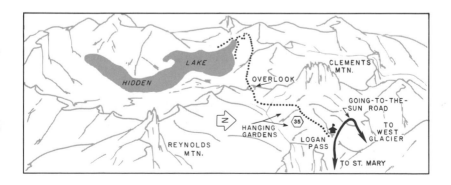

Mountain goat; McDonald Creek valley in background

36 The Garden Wall

One way to The Loop: 11.8 miles (18.9 km)
Elevation gain: 800 feet (244 m)
High point: 7200 feet (2195 m)
Hiking time: 7 hours
Day hike or backpack

Round trip to Granite Park: 15.2 miles (24.3 km)
Elevation gain: 800 feet (244 m)
High point: 7200 feet (2195 m)
Hiking time: 8 hours
Day hike or backpack

If you have just one whole day to devote to hiking in Glacier National Park, walk the Highline Trail along the Garden Wall to Granite Park. On this hike you will walk through flower-covered meadows and glacier-carved basins, pass bubbling creeks, and view ice-sculpted mountains. Wildlife abounds, and chances are good of seeing anything from ground squirrels and marmots to mountain goats, bighorn sheep, and, of course, grizzly bears.

There are several ways to approach this hike. If you are in good shape, the entire distance from Logan Pass to Granite Park and back can be hiked in one very long day. The popular alternative is a one-way hike to Granite Park, followed by a descent to The Loop on the Going-to-the-Sun Road. The shuttle bus offers a convenient way to return to the Logan Pass trailhead. A third option is to spend a night at a backcountry campground for backpackers that is located in Granite Park. However, in July and August this popular camp-site is open only to hikers on extended trips.

One of the highlights of the Granite Park area is a beautiful old chalet. Until 1993, when the chalet was closed indefinitely for re-pairs, meals were served to day hikers and overnight lodging was provided to anyone with reservations. For further information, con-tact Glacier National Park (see the Useful Addresses section).

Access: Drive the Going-to-the-Sun Road to Logan Pass and park at the summit (elevation 6680 feet). The trail begins across the road, opposite the parking lot entrance.

The Hike: The trail has a spectacular beginning, first travers-ing the meadows above the road, then cutting across cliffs on a nar-row ledge where a cable has been hung for security.

At 2.2 miles the trail winds through a glacier-carved basin, then climbs to a small pass between Mount Gould and Haystack Butte. Hikers arriving in this area at midday may have the oppor-tunity to watch the mountain goats on their daily trek from the open slopes of the Garden Wall to the shade of Haystack Butte.

The next couple of miles are spent traversing a steep hillside, passing from one small meadow to the next. The Livingston Range comes into view, as does the Granite Park Chalet. At 6.8 miles pass a spur trail to the Grinnell Glacier Overlook that climbs 1000 feet in just 0.8 mile. At 7.6 miles the trail divides. The right fork climbs to the chalet, and the left fork descends 3.7 miles to The Loop.

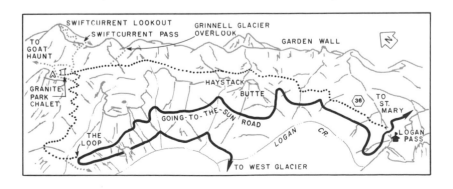

MANY GLACIER

The Indian name for the Swiftcurrent Creek valley meant "waterfalls." The white man renamed it Many Glacier, but unless someone can coin a word that encompasses superb alpine scenery, glacier-carved mountains, fifteen lakes, miles of meadows, a profusion of flowers, and an abundance of wildlife, as well as glaciers and waterfalls, it must be admitted that no word in the English or the Blackfeet languages can truly describe this outstanding area.

Swiftcurrent Lake, Many Glacier Hotel, and Wynn Mountain

Accommodations And Services

The huge Many Glacier Hotel, scenically located on the shores of Swiftcurrent Lake, and the Swiftcurrent Motor Inn, with its motel units and rustic cabins, are the accommodations in the Many Glacier area. The hotel and motor inn are run by Glacier Park, Inc., and are booked for months ahead (see the Where to Stay section in the Introduction for details). The closest accommodations outside the park is a small motel in Babb, 11 miles to the east.

The Many Glacier Campground is open for full operation from mid-June to late September. Primitive camping, without running water, is allowed in the fall until the area is closed by snow. The campground has 112 sites, 13 of which can accommodate RVs up to 35 feet long. In midsummer there is a campfire program every night. The campground is usually full by noon in July and August, and late arrivers should plan to spend the night outside the park at one of the two KOA campgrounds on Lower St. Mary Lake.

A small store near the campground has a supply of basic food, camping items, and fishing gear, as well as the usual souvenir assortment. Showers for you and washing machines and dryers for your clothes are available at the Swiftcurrent Motor Inn. Tokens may be purchased at the camp store or the front desk.

Food services are available at the Many Glacier Hotel dining room and snackbar. The Swiftcurrent Motor Inn has a coffee shop.

The Many Glacier Ranger Station, located next to the campground entrance, is open from mid-June through late September, from 8:00 A.M. to 4:30 P.M. Backpacking permits are issued there.

Activities

Bear watching is one of the most popular activities in the Many Glacier area. The open, grassy hillsides along the road are a popular feeding ground for grizzlies. Avid bear watchers may sight one or more foraging on the open slopes of the valley in the morning or late afternoon. If sighting a bear is on your wish list, carry binoculars and stop frequently to scan the hillsides as you drive up the valley from Babb.

In addition to bear, wildlife watchers may spot deer, elk, moose, mice, mountain sheep, and mountain goats in the valley or on the cliffs and ledges above.

The scenic boat tours at Many Glacier are the most entertaining in the park. The boat departs from the Many Glacier Hotel dock and crosses Swiftcurrent Lake. Passengers disembark on the far side of the lake and take a short walk through the forest to Lake Josephine, where a second boat completes the tour. Park naturalists are on board selected trips to point out the scenic highlights and answer questions. Tickets for the boat tours can be purchased at the ticket booth located near the Many Glacier Hotel.

Boat-and-hike tours offer a fun and easy way to explore the Many Glacier area. Take the boat to the upper end of Lake Josephine, then head out for a hike by yourself or with a boat guide or a ranger. In July and August there is a special early-morning cruise for hikers taking the ranger-led walk to Grinnell Glacier. Rangers also guide two daily walks from the upper boat dock to Grinnell Lake.

Rowboats and canoes are available for rent from the Many Glacier Hotel dock. Private canoes, rowboats, windsurfers, or kayaks may be launched from the east side of Swiftcurrent Lake.

Horseback rides here, starting from the Many Glacier Corral, are among the most scenic in the park. The corral, open from mid-June through mid-September, offers 1-hour, 2-hour, 3-hour, and all-

Bighorn sheep

day rides to places such as an old mining community on Cracker Flats, Cracker Lake, Poia Lake, and Granite Park Chalet.

Nature walks with a park ranger are offered every day at Many Glacier. The boat-and-hike trips to Grinnell Glacier and Grinnell Lake are the most popular outings. Some Grinnell Glacier trips include a walk on the ice to check out the ice caves and peer into the crevasses. There is also a walk to Iceberg Lake several times a week. Check at the ranger station for dates and times.

Short Hikes

Apikuni Falls. A 1.6-mile round trip on a steep trail with an 880-foot elevation gain leads to a pretty falls located at the edge of alpine meadows. A rough way-trail continues on from the falls, climbing over a band of cliffs to Natahki Lakes, a hike suitable only for the sure-footed. The trail begins at the Grinnell Glacier Exhibit, located 1.1 miles east of the Many Glacier Hotel.

Swiftcurrent Lake. A 2.4-mile self-guided nature trail loops the entire lake. Begin the walk from the south end of Many Glacier Hotel or at the Many Glacier Picnic Area. Pamphlets are available at both trailheads and at the ranger station.

Lake Josephine. This 2-mile round-trip hike, with an elevation gain of just 80 feet, has views of two lakes. Begin at the Many Glacier Picnic Area, located 0.7 mile west of the Many Glacier Hotel. Walk around Swiftcurrent Lake to the first intersection and go right, over a low hill, to the Lake Josephine boat dock.

Fishercap Lake. A round trip of just 0.5 mile, with only minor elevation gain, takes you to a lake where moose, elk, and deer may be seen. The trail begins at the end of the Many Glacier Road. Follow the Swiftcurrent Pass Trail for 0.1 mile to the lake trail intersection, go left, and descend to the lake. Fishing is reportedly poor.

Redrock Lake and Falls. This 3.4-mile round trip has only 100 feet of elevation gain. The trail begins at the end of the Many Glacier Road and follows the Swiftcurrent Pass Trail to Redrock Lake and Falls; the falls and the lake are located in a band of crimson red rock.

Ptarmigan Falls. This 5-mile round trip gains only 500 feet of elevation. Meadows, wildflowers, and views make this the most scenic short hike in this area. The trail begins at the end of the Many Glacier Road. Follow the Iceberg Lake–Ptarmigan Lake Trail to the falls.

Day Hikes And Backpacks

37 Cracker Lake

Round trip: 11.2 miles (17.9 km)
Elevation gain: 1140 feet (347 m)
High point: 5950 feet (1658 m)
Hiking time: 6 hours
Day hike or backpack

The turquoise blue color of Cracker Lake is startling in its intensity. On a cloudy day, the lake water has an iridescent glow that seems to fill the entire basin. On clear days, the color is so deep and rich that the lake looks like stained glass.

In a park with more than 250 lakes, Cracker Lake ranks as one of the most eye-catching. It is sandwiched between cliffs that rise 3000 feet in a single pitch. Waterfalls lace the hillsides, and delicate meadows surround the lake with a few clumps of stunted subalpine firs to complete the scene.

Access: Drive the Many Glacier Road 11.4 miles from the Highway 89 intersection at Babb. Go left at the Many Glacier Hotel turnoff and left again when the road divides. Park near the horse corral (elevation 4890 feet).

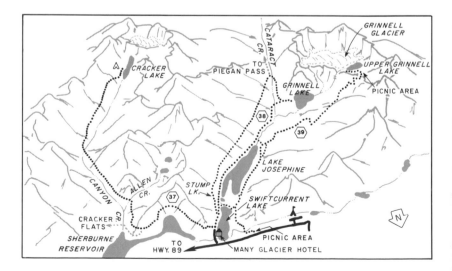

Cracker Lake

The Hike: Walk to the end of the parking lot to find the trailhead. After 50 feet the trail divides; the Piegan Pass Trail continues straight and the Cracker Lake Trail goes to the left and descends gradually to the muddy shores of Sherburne Reservoir.

Once the trail reaches lake level it begins a gradual climb along the edge of Cracker Flats. A horse trail branches off left at 1.5 miles to loop through the flats around an old mining townsite. The crossing of Allen Creek at 1.7 miles marks the beginning of the climb into the Canyon Creek valley on a series of well-graded switchbacks. The next landmark is Canyon Creek, which is crossed at 3.5 miles.

The climb continues, gradual but steady, through a thinning forest. At 5.6 miles the trail reaches the lake and divides. Stay left along the east side of the lake to reach the backcountry camp area. Shortly beyond, the trail passes some old machinery, abandoned by workmen at the Cracker Mine. The mine shaft is still there, but it is very dangerous to enter. You can walk all the way around the lake traversing the open meadows and grassy hillsides, then cross Canyon Creek at the lake outlet to return to the main trail.

Angel Wing towering above Grinnell Lake

38 Grinnell Lake

Round trip: 6.8 miles (10.9 km)
Elevation gain: 72 feet (22 m)
High point: 4950 feet (1509 m)
Hiking time: 4 hours
Day hike

When hiking to Grinnell Lake, you can choose between a cool walk through the shady forest or a scenic traverse over rocky avalanche slopes with views of the entire valley. Or you can be creative and mix the two routes to make interesting combinations, such as a loop hike or a crazy figure-eight.

However, if you prefer a lazy day, with more basking in the sun at the lakeshore than walking, ride the tour boats up Swiftcurrent Lake and Lake Josephine. The resulting hike is a 1.8-mile round trip with virtually no elevation gain.

Access: With all these options, there is more than one place to begin your hike. For the boat-and-hike option, the trip begins from the Many Glacier Hotel. You may also begin your hike from the hotel by walking down to the lakeshore or up to the horse corral. The other popular starting point is at the Grinnell Glacier trailhead in the Many Glacier Picnic Area. **(See map on page 150.)**

The Hike: For a cool walk through the shady forest, start from the Many Glacier Hotel and walk down to the lakeshore. Follow the Swiftcurrent Lakeshore Nature Trail south, up the lake. When the trail divides, stay left and walk by tiny Stump Lake and then along the forested east shore of Lake Josephine to Grinnell Lake.

The scenic traverse over avalanche slopes begins at the Many Glacier Picnic Area and follows the Grinnell Glacier Trail around the west side of Swiftcurrent Lake. When the trail divides, go right and climb a short rise, then traverse the west side of Lake Josephine. Views extend up the lake to Mount Gould, Bishop's Cap, and Cataract Mountain. Near the upper end of Lake Josephine, bear left, following the boardwalk past the upper tour boat dock. The trail then parallels Cataract Creek to Grinnell Lake.

A third and somewhat longer route begins at the horse corral. Follow the Piegan Pass Trail to the Grinnell Lake turnoff, then descend to the lake. This route offers views of Grinnell Glacier and Lake Josephine.

Located in a deep cirque, Grinnell Lake is picture-perfect. At the far end of the lake, Grinnell Falls plunges down the cliffs. The lakeshore is great for picnicking. Trout can be lured from the depths of the lake by wily fishermen. For the explorers, a rough path traverses around the southeastern side of the lake to the base of the falls.

39 Grinnell Glacier

Round trip: 11 miles (17.6 km)
Elevation gain: 1698 feet (518 m)
High point: 6560 feet (1585 m)
Hiking time: 6 hours
Day hike

If you have never had an up-close look at a glacier, this hike offers the opportunity to take a look at crevasses, moats, bergschrunds, snowbridges, nunataks, ice caves, and moraines. If you

Grinnell Glacier Trail

have had plenty of experience with glaciers, then take this hike to enjoy the outstanding scenery.

The Grinnell Glacier is an excellent hike from start to finish. However, if time is limited or the distance seems like more than you want to tackle, the trip can be shortened with a boat ride up Swiftcurrent and Josephine lakes.

The boat-and-hike combination is a 7.6-mile round trip, with about the same amount of elevation gain.

Access: The Grinnell Glacier Trail begins at the Many Glacier Picnic Area (elevation 4878 feet), located 0.7 mile west of the Many Glacier Hotel. **(See map on page 150.)**

The Hike: Begin your hike by following the Swiftcurrent Lake Nature Trail around the west side of the lake. At the upper end of Swiftcurrent Lake is a junction; go right and climb over a short hill on a paved trail.

At 0.8 mile from the picnic area, the trail divides again; take the right fork and head up the north side of Lake Josephine, enjoying views of the lake and the Angel Wing at the head of the valley.

Views on this portion of the trail are expansive, and one wonders how they can improve, but they do.

Near the upper end of the lake, stay right at two junctions. The trail now begins to climb, traversing steep ledges to reach the alpine meadows on the side of Mount Grinnell. Below lies Grinnell Lake. Morning Eagle Falls comes into view below Bishop's Cap, and the trail to Piegan Pass can be seen switchbacking up the rocky talus slopes of Cataract Mountain.

In the early summer, water streams off Mount Grinnell, tumbling beside and often over the trail in roaring cascades and lacy waterfalls, cooling the brow and dampening the feet.

At 5 miles is a tiny meadow with a few windswept trees. This is the site of the Grinnell Picnic Area and the end of the formal trail. From this point you must follow a rough route over the talus. It is worth the effort to scramble to the top of the moraine for a close-up view of ice-strewn Upper Grinnell Lake and the glacier.

For most hikers the lake is the turnaround point. However, if you must touch the ice, go left. Head over the rocks, creeks, and occasional block of ice, and pass the lake outlet to the glacier. Do not walk on the glacier: the crevasses are deep and a fall would be deadly. If you are interested in exploring the ice, do so in the company of a park naturalist. Check at the ranger station for the dates and times of the glacier tours.

40 Iceberg Lake

Round trip: 9.4 miles (15 km)
Elevation gain: 1219 feet (372 m)
High point: 6094 feet (1857 m)
Hiking time: 5 hours
Day hike

On a warm summer day, hikers crowd the shore of Iceberg Lake. They come to watch the sunlight dance across the icebergs floating in the chalky blue, glacier-fed waters. They sit for hours, entranced by the fanciful shapes of the floating ice and contemplating the 3000-foot cliff that rises straight out of the lake, like a giant cathedral wall.

The trail to Iceberg Lake is very popular. The tread is wide and the grade gradual. Experienced hikers will find this an easy hike, novices will find it enjoyable, and everyone will be impressed by the scenery.

Access: Drive to the end of the Many Glacier Road. Just past the general store, turn right on a narrow road that winds around the motor inn's cabins. Stay left and follow the signs to the Iceberg Lake trailhead parking area (elevation 4885 feet).

The Hike: The trail begins with a couple of well-signed intersections, first with the Swiftcurrent Pass Trail (stay right), then with the Many Glacier Hotel Trail (stay left).

The Iceberg Lake Trail starts off with a steep climb, gaining 200 feet of elevation before settling into a long, gradual traverse over the open slopes of Mount Henkel. The views begin at the trailhead. Before long there is a panoramic look up the Swiftcurrent Creek valley, all the way to Swiftcurrent Pass and the Swiftcurrent Mountain Lookout. A profusion of wildflowers covers the open hillside below and above the trail. Mountain sheep and an occasional bear may be seen.

At 2.8 miles the trail enters the forest and crosses Ptarmigan Creek, just above Ptarmigan Falls. Not long after, the trail divides. The right-hand trail heads up through the Ptarmigan Tunnel to the Belly River area (see trip 44). The left fork leads to Iceberg Lake.

The trail continues its traverse and gradual climb under a great barrier of cliffs known as the Ptarmigan Wall. After the forest ends

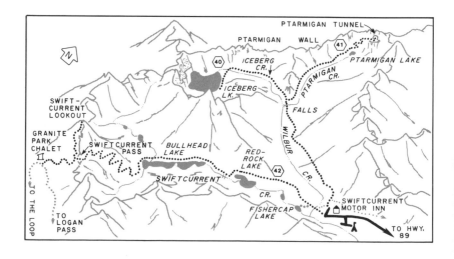

Iceberg Lake and Iceberg Peak

at 3.2 miles, the remainder of the hike is over open slopes with entrancing views of the valley.

Cross Iceberg Creek at 4.5 miles, then climb through fragile alpine meadows for the final 0.2 mile. Rocks at the edge of the lake make excellent seats for a picnic lunch, but watch out for the squirrels that appear like magic at the same time your sandwich comes out of the pack. Don't feed these cute little creatures: our food may kill them.

41 Ptarmigan Tunnel

Round trip: 11.2 miles (17.9 km)
Elevation gain: 2315 feet (706 m)
High point: 7200 feet (2195 m)
Hiking time: 6 hours
Day hike

The objective of this hike is a tunnel that was cut through the solid rock of the Ptarmigan Wall. Although this novelty may be the inspiration that gets most hikers to the trailhead, it's the spectacular scenery that motivates the legs on the long climb.

Mount Wilbur viewed from inside Ptarmigan Tunnel

Elizabeth Lake and Belly River valley north of Ptarmigan Tunnel

Access: Drive to the end of the Many Glacier Road and park (elevation 4885 feet). **(See map on page 156.)**

The Hike: Start the hike from the end of the parking area by following the Swiftcurrent Pass Trail for 100 feet. Go right at the first intersection and walk past the Swiftcurrent Motor Inn. The trail climbs steeply at first, gaining 200 feet in 0.2 mile. In this section two more intersections are passed; stay left at both.

After the second intersection the trail begins a long traverse across the open flanks of Altyn Peak and Mount Henkel. Wildflowers, wildlife, and views all vie for your attention. Keep alert: bears frequently cross these open slopes, hunting for berries or small rodents. You may also see deer or mountain sheep on the rocks above.

At 2.8 miles, the trail enters the forest, then crosses Ptarmigan Creek at the top of Ptarmigan Falls. A short distance beyond, the trail divides. To the left is Iceberg Lake (see trip 40). Ptarmigan Lake and the tunnel are to the right.

Ascend, first through forest, then over meadows with views of Ptarmigan Wall and Crowfeet Mountain to inspire weary feet. After paralleling Ptarmigan Creek for 1.6 miles, reach the end of the valley and Ptarmigan Lake. Follow the trail as it swings around the lake, then heads steadily up an open scree slope to the tunnel (elevation 7200 feet).

No hike would be complete without a walk through the 183-foot-long tunnel to check out the view on the north side of the Ptarmigan Wall. Elizabeth Lake is 2300 feet below. Beyond lies the Belly River country, an area worth more than just a casual glance from this vantage point.

42 Swiftcurrent Pass

Round trip to Granite Park Chalet: 15.2 miles (24.3 km)
Elevation gain: 2315 feet in (706 m); 545 feet out (166 m)
High point: 7195 feet (2193 m)
Hiking time: 8 hours
Day hike or backpack

Round trip to lookout: 15.6 miles (25 km)
Elevation gain: 3556 feet (1084 m)
High point: 8436 feet (2571 m)
Hiking time: 9 hours
Day hike

This is one of those rare trails that have so many points of interest, a short hike can be as enjoyable as a long one. Pick your destination from a list that includes four lakes, waterfalls, several vista points, a high alpine basin, a pass on the Continental Divide, and a lookout with the best panoramic view in the entire park.

The Granite Park Chalet is closed until at least 1996. The camping situation may also pose a problem; in the busy months of July and August, the Granite Park backcountry camp area, the only camp near this trail, is open, though only to hikers on extended trips.

Access: From the Highway 89 junction at Babb, drive the Many Glacier Road for 12 miles to its end. The Swiftcurrent Pass Trail begins at the far end of the parking lot (elevation 7195 feet). **(See map on page 156.)**

The Hike: Heading up the Swiftcurrent Creek valley, the first point of interest is Wilbur Creek. Soon after is a junction with the trail to forested Fishercap Lake.

Climb gradually under a leafy arbor of aspens to a rocky out-

View of lake-dotted Swiftcurrent Creek valley from Swiftcurrent Pass Trail

crop. From this point on the country is open and the ground cover is predominantly grass, with a few mountain willows and stunted subalpine firs to add some texture to the scene.

Redrock Lake, at 1.3 miles, is aptly named. Surrounded by deep crimson rock, the lake is strikingly beautiful. At the end of the lake is Redrock Falls, an excellent destination for short hikes.

Climb to the crest of a red rock rib (argillite), then continue up-valley, passing an unnamed lake before reaching Bullhead Lake at 2.5 miles. Up to this point there has been very little elevation gain; however, just beyond the lake the trail begins to climb and in the next 3.5 miles gains 2000 feet.

A grassy knoll above Bullhead Lake is the first of many vista points overlooking the Swiftcurrent Creek valley. Beyond the knoll, the valley ends in a cirque, where as many as eight waterfalls could be dancing down the cliffs. The trail comes close to one of these waterfalls, then switchbacks and traverses a narrow ledge to reach a small alpine basin. After crossing a lively creek the trail divides; the old and new trails cut parallel courses into a higher basin. The final climb is through an oasis of alpine meadows.

At 6.6 miles reach the crest of 7195-foot Swiftcurrent Pass and cross the Continental Divide. From the pass it's a 1-mile descent to Granite Park Chalet and 2 miles to the camp area. Energetic hikers are strongly encouraged to make the steep, 1241-foot climb from the pass to the lookout at the crest of Swiftcurrent Mountain. The panoramic view is unbelievable. Two points of caution: Avoid Swiftcurrent Mountain on windy days, and do not venture too far on the north side of the lookout, where there is nothing but cliffs and a long drop to the bottom.

43 The Northern Circle

Loop trip: 55.8 miles (89.3 km)
Elevation gain: 8108 feet (2471 m)
High point: 7440 feet (2268 m)
Hiking time: 5–7 days
Backpack

Hike a loop through the wilderness of the northeast corner of the park where more than half the trail is above timberline. The scenery is outstanding as the trail heads from panoramic vistas to beautiful lakes, past waterfalls and rivers, to high alpine meadows

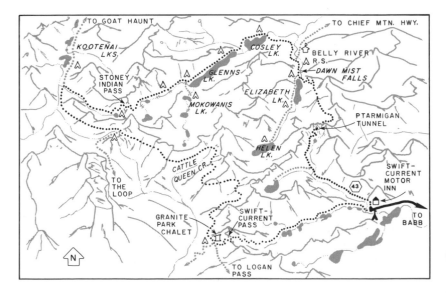

and lovely fields of wildflowers. Wildlife is abundant in the mountainous terrain traversed on this loop, and the observant hiker may see bears, elk, deer, and moose. Mountain lions roam the valleys, as do lynx. Hawks, eagles, and owls have been spotted in the forest and mountains, while numerous ducks, geese, and loons have been seen, and heard, on the lakes.

Because this is a beautiful and popular area, backcountry permits may be hard to get. Plan to apply for your permit at 8:00 A.M. the day before you intend to start your hike. Arrive at the backcountry desk with two itineraries in hand, one for clockwise and one for counterclockwise. If the campsites are full in one direction, hopefully there will be space the other way.

Access: The loop begins from the end of the Many Glacier Road, 12 miles west of Babb (elevation 4885 feet). The following description is for a counterclockwise loop.

The Hike: On day one, hikers are faced with a mandatory 9.9 mile walk from Many Glacier to Elizabeth Lake, where the first backcountry campsite is located. This is a long walk for most hikers with packs bulging with supplies for the trip. From the parking area, hike to Ptarmigan Tunnel (see trip 41), then descend to find a large camp area at the outlet of the lake.

After the first day, there are more campsites to choose from, and the next couple of days can be tailored to fit the time and energy constraints of the hiker. From Elizabeth Lake it's a gentle descent to Dawn Mist Falls, followed by a gradual climb to reach Cosley Lake at 3.9 miles. The loop turns to the southwest here and heads up the Mokowanis River valley to Stoney Indian Pass. At the base of Cosley Lake is a campsite; the next is located 1.5 miles up-valley at the lower end of Glenns Lake, and a third is located 4.3 miles up-valley at the head of Glenns Lake. Just 0.6 mile beyond is the Mokowanis Junction Camp. The trail passes several small tarns, a waterfall, and a lovely cascade on its way to 6908-foot Stoney Indian Pass, located 9.5 miles from Cosley Lake Camp.

From the pass the trail switchbacks down to Stoney Indian Lake Camp, then continues down to the Pass Creek junction, 3.5 miles below the pass. The loop turns south and heads up Kootenai Creek, climbing for 5.6 miles to the high open country and to the next campsite, at Fifty Mountain. This is a beautiful location, and most loop hikers will want to spend a night here. The next campsite is at Granite Park, 11.9 miles to the east.

Dawn Mist Falls

From Fifty Mountain Camp, the loop route follows the Highline Trail. This section is almost entirely above timberline, with the full expanse of the Livingston Range spread out for viewing to the west. The trail reaches the 7440-foot high point of the loop on a shoulder of Mount Kipp, descends to below 6000 feet at Cattle Queen Creek, then climbs back up to 6800 feet by the end of the day.

From Granite Park, there are no more camp areas on the loop, so the final 7.9 miles over Swiftcurrent Pass must be completed in a single day. This last leg of the circle is relatively easy, with 1 mile of climbing and 6.9 miles of descent to Many Glacier.

If time allows there are several excellent side trips to be made off the basic circle, to Helen Lake, Mokowanis Lake, Kootenai Lakes, and the Swiftcurrent Mountain Lookout.

44 Belly River

Round trip to Belly River campground: 12.4 miles (19.8 km)
Elevation gain: 80 feet in (24 m); 809 feet out (247 m)
High point: 5329 feet (1624 m)
Hiking time: 6 hours
Day hike or backpack

Designed for backpackers by Mother Nature herself, the Belly River valley is a perfect hike with very little elevation gain and outstanding views.

Although Belly River is an easy day hike, it takes 3 to 5 days to

Dried, cracked mud

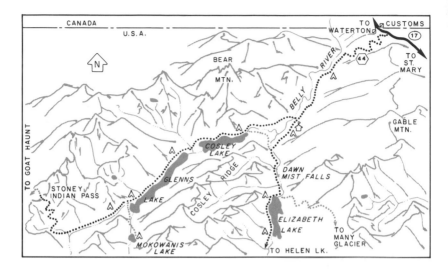

explore this area. The longer stays allow you enough time to hike to the Belly River Campground and set up a base camp, then spend the next couple of days exploring on up the Belly River valley to Dawn Mist Falls, Elizabeth Lake, and Helen Lake, or to Cosley and Glenns lakes in the Mokowanis River valley.

Before heading to the trailhead, pick up a backcountry camping permit. Permits are *not* issued in the Belly River area. Hikers without a permit may unable to find an open campsite forced to leave the area. They may also be fined.

Access: From St. Mary, drive Highway 89 north for 12 miles, then turn left onto Highway 17 (Chief Mountain International Highway) and drive 14.4 miles. The trailhead is located 500 feet from the Chief Mountain border crossing (elevation 5329 feet).

The Hike: The trail begins with a 2-mile-long, 809-foot descent to the valley floor. Due to a combination of heavy horse traffic and clay soil, the trail can be very muddy after a rain. Walk carefully to avoid slipping when the trail is wet.

Follow an old wagon road up the valley through aspen groves and grassy meadows (be prepared for lots of mosquitoes here). At 3 miles, the trail brushes the edge of the Belly River, providing a choice location for the Three Mile backcountry campground.

Continuing up the valley, cross one grassy meadow after another with views of Chief Mountain, Gable Mountain, Cosley Ridge, and Sentinel and Bear mountains. At 6.2 miles the trail encounters a fancy wooden fence, signaling your arrival at the Belly River

Ranger Station. The trail divides here. The first junction is with the Stoney Indian Pass Trail, which branches off on the right, heading to Cosley Lake (2.5 miles), Glenns Lake (4 miles), Mokowanis Lake (8 miles), and Stoney Indian Pass (12 miles). This trail descends directly to the Belly River and crosses on a suspension bridge that is removed for the winter by mid-September.

The second junction is with the trail to the ranger station. Stay to the right here and walk around the corral to find the trail to the campground at the far end of the meadow. The Belly River camp area is located on a bend of the river in the shadow of Bear Mountain, Cosley Ridge, and Gable Mountain.

The Belly River Trail continues upriver, crossing to the west bank at 7.8 miles where it joins an alternate trail from Cosley Lake. At 8.2 miles a short side trail branches left to the base of the impressive Dawn Mist Falls.

At 9.8 miles the trail arrives at the foot of Elizabeth Lake, where there is a backcountry campsite and a junction with the Ptarmigan Tunnel Trail. A second campsite is located at the head of Elizabeth Lake, at 11.2 miles. The Belly River Trail ends at 13.6 miles in a narrow cirque where beautiful Helen Lake lies at the base of Ahern Peak, receiving much of its water and all of its distinctive coloring from the Ahern Glacier.

Belly River valley

GOAT HAUNT

Beginning long before man began recording his journeys, people have been visiting the upper end of Waterton Lake: first Indians, then trappers, next loggers and hunters, and finally tourists. The Indians came and went for thousands of years, leaving very little mark on the area. However, since his arrival less then 200 years ago, the white man has greatly impacted this area, hunting the goats to near extinction and constructing a road to haul logs over the mountains. A lodge was built at Goat Haunt to house tourists who traveled across Glacier National Park on horses.

Times change. Goat Haunt became part of Glacier National Park in 1910. In 1962 the lodge was swept away in a flood, and the Park Service did not rebuild. Today, neither food nor lodging is available to the visitor at Goat Haunt.

Despite the endless stream of visitors down through the centuries, the back door of the Goat Haunt Ranger Station still opens to some of the most isolated wilderness in Glacier National Park.

Accommodations And Services

Goat Haunt is basically a backcountry ranger station with a few extras such as the International Peace Pavilion, where naturalists give talks and visitors can learn to identify wildflowers and animal tracks. A second pavilion provides historical insights into the area. Visitors can get trail information and climbing or backcountry camping permits at the shoebox-size ranger station.

(Note: Permits are issued at Goat Haunt on a space-available basis. If you wait until you reach Goat Haunt to apply for your backcountry camping permit, you may find yourself heading back down the lake on the same boat you came up on. Apply for your permit in Glacier National Park. Do not make the mistake of trying to obtain backcountry camping permits for the Goat Haunt area when you reach Waterton.)

There are two campsites in the immediate vicinity of Goat Haunt and two more within easy hiking distance. The Goat Haunt shelters are the closest, located right next to the boat dock. This

Olson Mountain (right), Porcupine Ridge (left), and Waterton Lake near Goat Haunt

unique camp has three-sided structures with cement floors for protection against the wind and rain. If you use a tent here, it needs to be a self-standing one.

The Waterton River campsite is located 0.8 mile from Goat Haunt on the Waterton Lakeshore Trail. This is a traditional backcountry campsite with tent sites and a food prep area. Lake Janet Camp, located on the Boulder Pass Trail, and Kootenai Lakes Camp, located on the Waterton Valley Trail, are two campsites located within walking distance (less than 4 miles) from Goat Haunt.

Goat Haunt is the only entry point to Glacier National Park that is not accessible by car. The easiest way to get there is by boat from the Waterton townsite in Canada. The boat makes several trips up Waterton Lake every day, spending about 30 minutes at Goat Haunt before heading back down the lake. However, you can write your own schedule. If you like, arrive in the morning and take the last boat back down the lake in the evening, or camp out and go back in a day or so. You can also hike to Goat Haunt from several points in Glacier or Waterton Lakes and catch the boat out by buying a one-way ticket, available in the town of Waterton Park or on the boat. The boat operates from mid-May to mid-September. Off-season visitors must use the trails.

It must be remembered that hikers accessing Goat Haunt from Waterton Park, or vice versa, are crossing an international boundary. The park ranger who greets the boats at Goat Haunt is also a U.S. Customs official. Anyone arriving from Canada by boat or by foot must report to that ranger. If you go into Canada after hiking in Glacier National Park, you must fill out a simple form and make a toll-free call to the customs officials. If you carry some form of identification when you hike, you should not have any problems crossing the international border.

Activities

There is a lot to do and see at Goat Haunt. If you only have an hour or so, try one of the two short hikes listed below. If you have the entire day, consider a hike to Kootenai Lakes (see trip 45), or head up the Boulder Pass Trail to Lake Janet or Lake Francis (see trip 46). Of course, you can always head back to the Waterton townsite on the Waterton Lakeshore Trail (see trip 48). There are ranger-guided walks up the Goat Haunt Overlook several times a week during the summer season and a guided walk along the Waterton Lakeshore Trail once a week. Check at any ranger station in Glacier National Park for dates and times.

Short Hikes

Goat Haunt Overlook. There is an excellent view of Waterton Lake and the Olson Creek valley from the crest of a knoll just east of Goat Haunt. It is a 2-mile round-trip hike with a steep climb, gaining 700 feet of elevation in 1 mile. Walk from the boat dock to the ranger station, then follow the Kootenai Lakes Trail for 200 feet. The trail to the overlook begins behind the rangers' bunk house.

Rainbow Falls. Located on the Waterton River, the falls is an easy 2-mile round trip with only 80 feet of elevation gain. From the boat dock, walk to the ranger station, then follow the Waterton Lakeshore Trail. After 0.3 mile the trail divides; go left and walk through the forest for another 0.7 mile to the falls.

Day Hikes And Backpacks

45 Kootenai Lakes

Round trip: 5 miles (8 km)
Elevation gain: 200 feet (61 m)
High point: 4400 feet (1341 m)
Hiking time: 3 hours
Day hike or backpack

Standing around 5 feet tall at the shoulder and weighing nearly 700 pounds, the moose is an impressive mammal. The antlers are massive, its legs are long, and each hoof covers almost as much area as the human foot.

It is the chance to watch moose in their natural habitat that brings so many hikers to the Kootenai Lakes in the marshy Waterton Valley. Backpackers who spend a night at the Kootenai Lakes backcountry campground have a good chance of seeing moose in the early-morning or evening hours. Even observant day hikers occasionally spot a moose while walking in the vicinity of the lakes.

Access: Obtain your backcountry camping permit in Glacier National Park, then drive north to the Waterton townsite and either catch the boat up the lake or walk the Waterton Lakeshore Trail to Goat Haunt.

The Hike: From the Goat Haunt Ranger Station (elevation 4196 feet), follow the Waterton River Trail through the residential area. After a few feet the pavement ends and the trail becomes a

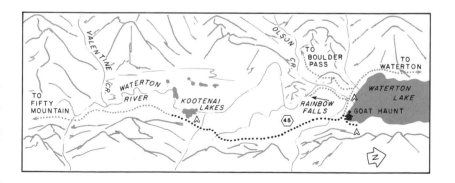

Moose

gravel road. When the road ends, continue up the nearly level Waterton Valley on a wide trail. The valley floor is forested, with an occasional marsh and small meadows to break the monotony. At 2.5 miles go right on a spur trail to the lakes.

The Kootenai Lakes are located in a section of the Waterton Valley where the river meanders in convoluted twists and broad turns. The valley has numerous lakes, meadows, and swamps. Beavers have added more ponds and marshes. It's an altogether ideal habitat for moose. Of course, bears, deer, and elk also inhabit this lush valley. Very lucky visitors may even see a lynx or cougar.

The Kootenai Lakes are surprisingly beautiful, surrounded by meadows, the towering Citadel Peaks, and Porcupine Ridge. Animal and boot-made trails wander to several lakes, all of which are worth exploring.

46 Boulder Pass Trail—East Side

Round trip to Lake Janet: 6 miles (9.6 km)
Elevation gain: 844 feet (257 m)
High point: 5040 feet (1536 m)
Hiking time: 3 hours
Day hike or backpack

Round trip to Boulder Pass: 26.4 miles (42.2 km)
Elevation gain: 2924 feet (891 m)
High point: 7120 feet (2170 m)
Hiking time: 2–3 days
Backpack

Beautiful meadows, colorful talus, mountains, glaciers, lakes, and extraordinary vistas make this one of the most popular backcountry hiking areas in Glacier National Park.

Access: Once you have that all-important backcountry use permit, drive to the Waterton townsite and take the tour boat to Goat Haunt. (Alternate access is via the 8.7-mile Waterton Lakeshore Trail from the Waterton townsite. See trip 48 for more information.)

The Hike: The hike begins at the Goat Haunt boat dock (elevation 4196 feet). Walk the paved trail along the lakeshore to the ranger station, then continue on for 20 feet to an intersection. Go right on the Waterton Lakeshore Trail, which heads into the forest, paralleling the Waterton River. At 0.3 mile, the Rainbow Falls Trail branches off to the left. Shortly after, cross the Waterton River on a suspension bridge. (The bridge is removed in the winter. Check bridge status in the spring and fall before starting out.)

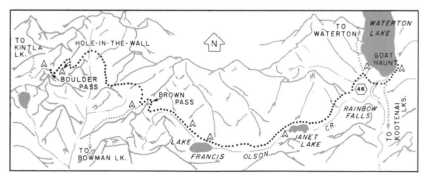

Citadel Peaks viewed from Lake Janet

Once across the Waterton River, a spur trail heads off on the right to the Waterton River camp. At 0.9 mile the Boulder Pass Trail leaves the Waterton Lakeshore Trail and heads left, to start its long climb to the high country.

The trail ascends through forest to reach Lake Janet at 2.8 miles. The small, forested Lake Janet campsite is located just above the lake.

Views are rare in the Olson Creek valley until you reach Lake Francis (elevation 5225 feet) at 6.2 miles. The Lake Francis camp area is located about halfway up the lake, and a second campsite, Hawksbill, is located 0.5 mile beyond the upper end of the lake.

Past the lake the forest thins and is soon replaced by lush meadows. At 7.2 miles a small pond marks the start of the final push to 6255-foot Brown Pass, which is reached at 8.6 miles. There is a campsite, located a short distance below the pass, on the Bowman Lake Trail.

Beyond Brown Pass, the climb continues as the trail traverses steep, open slopes on the side of Mount Chapman. The narrow trail was blasted into the rocky hillside, and the views are tremendous. At 10.3 miles a trail branches to the left, descending to the very scenic Hole-in-the-Wall backcountry camp area.

Boulder Pass (elevation 7410 feet) is reached at 13.6 miles, and the camp area is 0.5 mile farther on, in the basin beyond the pass.

WATERTON LAKES NATIONAL PARK

Goat Lake Trail and Bauerman Creek valley

The Waterton townsite is the heart of the activities, lodging, services, and administration of Waterton Lakes National Park. The townsite is a busy place during the summer months, and the streets seem to overflow with cars, RVs, tourists, cyclists, mountain sheep, deer, and an occasional bear.

The townsite is scenically located on a small delta, sandwiched between mountains and cliffs to the north and west and beautiful Upper Waterton Lake to the south and east. On a knoll just north of the townsite, the majestic Prince of Wales Hotel dominates the skyline.

With all the scenery and abundant wildlife, it is easy to overlook the one flaw in this paradise—the wind. It's a curious fact that all of the larger lakes of Waterton Lakes (and Glacier National Park too) are aligned with the mountains and act like funnels for the wind as it speeds from the cool, damp west side of the Rockies to the dry, warm eastern plains. The saying is: "The wind is not really blowing until there are whitecaps in the toilet bowls at the Prince of Wales Hotel." So come to the park prepared for wind. The wind is strongest along the shores of Upper Waterton Lake. Up in the side valleys, the mountains offer some protection until you reach the ridge tops. When heading out for a day in the park, carry a wind jacket, hat, and gloves.

Accommodations And Services

The best-known hotel in the park is the stately Prince of Wales; however, there are seven other motels in town. Make your reservations well in advance, as all accommodations are booked solid during the summer and the nearest metropolitan center with lodging is Cardston, located 43 km east of the park. The Alberta Tourism Office is a great resource for information and lodging. The toll-free number is (800) 661-8888. For reservations, write to the Waterton Chamber of Commerce, Waterton Park, AB T0K 2M0.

From fast food to formal dining, the Waterton townsite has a wide variety of restaurants. Just for fun, try the high tea served in the afternoons at the Prince of Wales Hotel.

The town has one small grocery store with a full selection of snack food, camping food, and backpacking supplies. The prices are a bit steep.

There are three campgrounds in Waterton Lakes National Park. The Waterton Townsite Campground has 238 sites; 95 are fully serviced for RVs. The campground has cold running water,

Prince of Wales Hotel overlooking Middle and Upper Waterton lakes

showers, cooking shelters, and wood split and ready to burn. Evening programs are offered at the indoor theater in July and August. The campground has a beautiful location near the lakeshore, but can be extremely windy. Do not leave your tent unattended unless it is firmly staked down.

Crandell Campground, located on the Red Rock Parkway, has 129 sites and no hook-ups. This area is sheltered by trees that provide some protection from the pervasive winds. The campground has running water, cooking shelters, and split wood for the cookstoves.

The Belly River Campground, located on the Chief Mountain International Highway, is the most primitive of the three areas. It has twenty-four sites, a cook shelter, split wood for the stoves, vault toilets, and a playground for the kids, and is an ideal area for tent campers. Most sites are sheltered from the wind.

Three private campgrounds are located near the park entrance. For details, inquire at the park Information Centre.

The Waterton townsite has two gas stations, a laundromat, a bike shop, a sporting goods store, a bookstore, a pharmacy, photo supplies, and souvenirs galore. A small bank, located in the Caribou Clothes Store, offers the best exchange rates.

Pat's Gas Station rents mountain bikes as well as surreys, scooters, and baby strollers. Bring your own helmets and other riding gear. Canoes, rowboats, and paddle boats may be rented at Cameron Lake.

Activities

The most popular park activity is taking scenic drives on the Akamina Parkway to Crandell Lake and on the Red Rock Parkway to Red Rock Canyon. The Akamina Parkway heads up a narrow valley where the first producing oil well in Alberta was drilled. The Red Rock Canyon Parkway follows scenic Blakiston Creek up a wide valley. The road passes several exhibits on the area's geological, historic, and prehistoric features as well as numerous vista points.

Another popular drive goes to the Buffalo Paddocks, located on Highway 6 just north of the park entrance. There is a short walk to an overlook and a road through the enclosure.

Sign depicting activities and services in Waterton Park townsite

International cruises on Upper Waterton Lake are also a popular activity. The narrated cruises are 2 hours long, including a 20-minute stopover at the Goat Haunt area in the United States. One-way tickets are available, allowing the cruise to be combined with a hike.

Private boats are allowed on Middle and Upper Waterton lakes. They may be launched in Upper Waterton Lake from behind the park administration building or in Middle Waterton Lake from the Linnet Lake area, just east of the Prince of Wales Hotel. Boat slips may be rented at the Emerald Bay Marina. Due to the winds, the use of canoes, kayaks, or rowboats is not recommended on the upper lake.

Alpine Stables, located east of town, offers rides to mountain lakes or over the prairies. Call ahead for reservations at (403) 859-2462.

For culture, visit the Heritage Centre in downtown Waterton Park, which has a small museum and art gallery.

Other activities include golfing on an eighteen-hole course with outstanding views, swimming in the heated municipal pool, playing tennis on the townsite's courts, rock climbing on the Bears Hump, scuba diving, and rafting the Belly River.

Short Hikes

Linnet Lake Loop. This is an easy 1-km loop on a paved trail around Linnet Lake. The wheelchair-accessible trail is located adjacent to the Middle Waterton Lake boat ramp.

Bears Hump. A strenuous 2.4-km round trip with a 200-meter elevation gain leads to one of the best views in the park. The trail begins at the Information Centre, opposite the Prince of Wales Hotel.

Townsite Trail. This is an easy 3.2-km loop along the shores of Upper Waterton Lake. Pick up the trail anywhere in town.

Lower Bertha Falls. The 5.8-km round trip to the falls, with only a 150-meter elevation gain, is one of the most popular walks in the park. See the Bertha Lake and Falls hike for directions.

Crandell Lake. This small, forested lake fringed with mountains can be accessed from 6.9 km up the Akamina Parkway or from the Crandell Campground on the Red Rock Parkway. From the Akamina Parkway, the lake is a 3.2-km round trip with a 100-meter elevation gain. From the campground, the lake is a 4.8-km round trip with a 100-meter elevation gain. Overnight camping is allowed at the lake.

Vimy Peak from summit of Bears Hump

Akamina Lake. This easy 1-km round-trip hike takes you to a small forested lake. The trail begins from the Cameron Lake parking lot at the end of the Akamina Parkway.

Cameron Lakeshore. This is an easy 3.2-km round-trip walk along the west shore of Cameron Lake to a small peninsula and viewpoint. The trail begins at the end of the Akamina Parkway.

Red Rock Canyon Loop. No one should miss this easy 0.7-km loop walk around Red Rock Canyon to view the colorful rock. The trail starts from the parking area at the end of the Red Rock Parkway. This area is frequented by mountain sheep.

Blakiston Falls. A scenic and easy 2.0-km round trip leads to a viewpoint of this impressive falls. The walk begins from the parking lot at the upper end of the Red Rock Parkway. Walk across the bridge, then go left.

Belly River. Starting at the far end of the Group Area at the Belly River Campground, an unsigned trail follows the old wagon road up-valley. The entire hike is a 6.4-km round trip with only minor elevation gain. Views begin at 2.4 km, and the trail ends in a brushy quagmire near the Canada–United States border at 3.2 km.

Day Hikes And Backpacks

47 Bertha Lake and Falls

Round trip to falls: 5.8 km (3.6 mi)
Elevation gain: 150 meters (429 ft)
High point: 1435 meters (4708 ft)
Hiking time: 2.5 hours
Day hike

Round trip to lake: 13.8 km (8.6 mi)
Elevation gain: 470 meters (1542 ft)
High point: 1755 meters (5758 ft)
Hiking time: 5 hours
Day hike or backpack

Legend has it that Bertha was one of the original settlers in the Waterton townsite. And even though the very resourceful Bertha was eventually put in jail for passing bad money, there is nothing counterfeit about the excellence of this hike to a waterfall and lake that bear her name.

Both the falls and the lake are popular destinations. Even nonhikers will find the walk to the falls a lot of fun on a broad trail with only moderate elevation gain, numerous viewpoints, and signs to explain the different vegetation. The falls are pretty, though not spectacular. However, the picnic tables and outhouse at the base of the falls make it an ideal location for lunch or afternoon tea.

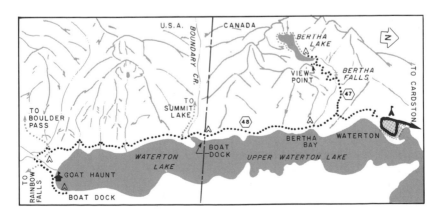

Beyond the falls the trail climbs a series of steep switchbacks. Beautiful subalpine Bertha Lake, in its deep valley, is worth the effort.

Access: The trail to Bertha Lake begins at the northwestern end of town. If you are arriving by car, drive past the turnoff to the Akamina Parkway, then head through town, staying right at all intersections. Pass Cameron Falls and continue 0.3 km to the Bertha Lake trailhead.

The Hike: Begin the hike by following the Waterton Lakeshore Trail along the west shore of the lake. Views start right away, first overlooking the townsite to Bears Hump, then extending across the lake to the rocky spires of Vimy Peak.

At 1.5 km, the trail divides. Leave the Waterton Lakeshore Trail and take the right fork up the Bertha Creek valley for another 1.4 km to Lower Bertha Falls. The falls is a fascinating area. Bertha Creek is a wide curtain of water when it plunges over the cliff. Then, at the base, the water funnels together to rush down a narrow channel cut into a layer of slanting strata.

If you are heading on to the lake, cross Bertha Creek, then begin the 4-km climb up the forested hillside, gaining 320 meters. At 6.8 km the trail divides. The left fork ends in 5 meters at a viewpoint overlooking Bertha Lake, Mount Alderson, and Mount Richards. The right fork descends steeply to the lakeshore. Continuing to the right, cross the outlet stream, to reach, in 0.2 km, the backcountry camp area, a picnic shelter with a large stove, and an outhouse. For those who want to explore, the trail can be followed around the entire lake.

48 Waterton Lakeshore Trail

One-way: 13.8 km (8.7 mi)
Elevation gain: 300 meters (984 ft)
High point: 1400 meters (4593 ft)
Hiking time: 5 hours
Day hike or backpack

Only two trails in Waterton–Glacier International Peace Park actually cross the border between the two countries. The unmaintained North Boundary Trail from Cameron Lake to Waterton Lake is one, and the Waterton Lakeshore Trail is the other.

Waterton Park townsite and Upper Waterton Lake

With an early start from the Waterton townsite, it is a relatively easy day hike to Goat Haunt, where you can catch the late-afternoon boat back and still have enough time for rest stops and a leisurely picnic lunch along the trail. Of course, the hike can be done in the other direction, with the boat ride first, and then the hike back down the lake. This second itinerary has the advantage of no schedule to follow. (Note: The tour boat runs from mid-May through mid-September.)

With the choice of four campsites along the lake, it is very easy to turn this trip into a 2- or 3-day adventure. (Note: Backcountry permits for the two U.S. camp areas must be obtained in Glacier National Park.)

Throughout the summer, a ranger from Glacier and a park interpreter from Waterton Lakes get together once a week to lead a hike along the lake. This is a great chance to learn about the flora, fauna, and the international aspects of the park while enjoying the company of a group as you walk from Waterton Park to Goat Haunt. Check at an Information Centre in either park for dates of these hikes.

Access: Drive to the Waterton townsite and park either at the Bertha Lake trailhead (see trip 47 for directions) or at the tour boat dock. From the tour boat dock, walk south along the lakeshore trail and follow signs to the Bertha Lake trailhead. **(See map on page 181.)**

The Hike: The lakeshore route begins as a nature trail, and as it climbs, plaques give descriptions of the vegetation. At 1.5 km the Bertha Lake Trail and most of the hikers head off to the right. Go left and descend to Bertha Bay and the first camp area. After crossing the small bay the trail heads back up. This is the first and perhaps the worst of the many descents and climbs you will make along the lake.

The most dramatic point of the hike is reached at 6.7 km, when the trail leaves the forest and crosses an 8-meter-wide swath that marks the international boundary between Canada and the United States. There is a small patrol cabin at the boundary (soon to be removed), as well as a backcountry campsite.

Walk across the border, pass a boat dock, then head away from the lake to cross Boundary Creek at 7.2 km. A short distance beyond is a junction with the North Boundary Trail. Continue straight.

The United States portion of the trail is forested, with few views. At 12 km a trail to the Waterton River campsite branches off on the left. The main trail turns right and heads away from the lake for 0.4 km to the Boulder Pass Trail intersection. Go left and cross the Waterton River on a suspension bridge, then pass the trail to Rainbow Falls (an excellent side trip if you have time to spare). The final 0.5 km is a pleasant forest ramble that ends at the Goat Haunt Ranger Station.

Walk the paved path along the lakeshore to the International Peace Pavilion, camping shelters, and the tour boat dock. On cool days, warm your feet at the large fire in the pavilion; on warm days, stick your feet in the lake while you wait for the boat.

49 Crypt Lake

Round trip: 17.2 km (10.8 mi)
Elevation gain: 634 meters (2080 ft)
High point: 1913 meters (6276 ft)
Hiking time: 6 hours
Day hike or backpack

To reach the shores of Crypt Lake, hikers take a boat ride, walk past several waterfalls, climb a ladder, crawl through a tunnel, and scale a cliff while hanging on to a very skinny cable.

This hike is not for everyone. If heights or vertigo are a problem, try one of the other excellent park trails. Younger children will have difficulties with the long steps at the entrance and exit of the tunnel. Parents who are accompanied by children may want to carry a 6-meter section of rope to secure the kids when they cross the exposed section of the cliff.

Access: A tour boat sails to Crypt Landing every morning, then returns for hikers in the late afternoon. Check at the Information Centre or the Emerald Bay boat dock for the current schedule.

The Hike: The trail begins at the Crypt Landing lakeside camp area. From the boat dock, go right and head up a series of switchbacks that take the trail over a shoulder of Vimy Peak and into the Hell-Roaring drainage. Along the way, two side trails are passed, one to Hell-Roaring Canyon and the other to Hell-Roaring

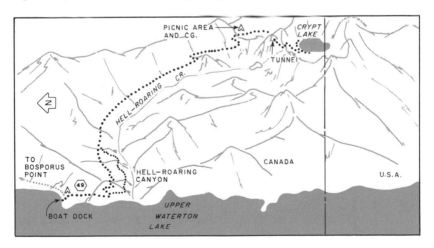

Crypt Lake trail near tunnel

Falls. These are actually two ends of the same trail. The Hell-Roaring Canyon/Falls Trail is steep and rough, and makes an interesting though slightly longer alternative descent.

Once in the Hell-Roaring drainage the trail parallels the creek for 2 km. Near the head of the valley you begin to climb again, first up a hillside of colorful rocks, then across subalpine meadows.

At 7.5 km, pass through a small backcountry campsite. Horses are left here, and the remainder of the trail is only for the sure-footed.

At this point there is only one band of cliffs between you and the lake. The trail crosses a boulder-strewn slope, then climbs into the tunnel with the help of a ladder. The tunnel is tight, so larger packs may have to be taken off and pushed through. On the far side of the tunnel, hikers must emulate mountain goats and scramble across a narrow pathway up the steep face of the cliff.

The lake is located in an upper cirque, just above the cliffs. The rocky shore provides an excellent location for a well-earned picnic. Ambitious hikers can walk around Crypt Lake, wandering from Canada to the United States and back to Canada.

50 Goat Lake

Round trip: 12.8 km (8 mi)
Elevation gain: 300 meters (984 ft)
High point: 2000 meters (6562 ft)
Hiking time: 5 hours
Day hike or backpack

At the base of Avion Ridge is a delicate subalpine lake surrounded on three sides by forest and meadows. The goats and sheep for which the lake was named live among the cliffs and scree slopes on the fourth side.

Hikers to Goat Lake are likely to see mountain goats or bighorn sheep on the ridge tops and hillsides, in the campground, or even on

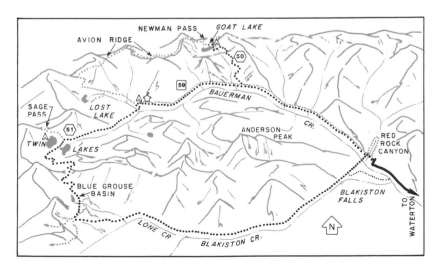

Bighorn sheep

the trail. These animals have become habituated to man's presence and spend a portion of their day looking for handouts and human salts. Please do not encourage them. Pack out every bit of your garbage and urinate only in the facilities provided.

Access: From the Waterton townsite, drive east for 3.1 km. Turn left on the Red Rock Parkway and follow it for 14.6 km to its end at a large parking lot (elevation 1500 meters).

The Hike: Walk across Red Rock Canyon on a sturdy bridge and continue straight at the trail junction on the other side. Boots pound the pavement for a short distance before the trail turns into an old fire road. Follow this road up the Bauerman Creek valley, through meadows and forest. There is a surprising number of viewpoints from the valley floor, and Anderson Peak and Mount Bauerman put on a handsome display.

The old road makes an excellent trail for the first couple of kilometers until it reaches an open area where the bridges have washed out and two creeks must be forded. Most of the year you can hop across on the boulders. However, in early summer you may get your feet wet.

After 3.9 km of relatively flat valley walking, the Goat Lake junction is reached. Go right and immediately begin to climb. In the next 2.5 km the trail gains more than 400 meters of elevation. At times the climb is so steep that a smoker will swear off the habit and a nonsmoker will sound like an asthmatic. After passing a couple of waterfalls the trail reaches Goat Lake at 6.4 km. The campsites are located in the meadow just above the lake.

If the spirit of the mountain goat is still within you, head on up to Avion Ridge for unobstructed views in every direction. The 1.6-km path to the ridge is considered to be a route rather than an official trail, which means that it can go straight up the hillside without bothering with switchbacks. Once on top, the energetic hiker can walk the open crest of Avion Ridge all the way to Lost Lake.

51 Twin Lakes Loop

Loop trip: 24.8 km (15.5 mi)
Elevation gain: 650 meters (2133 ft)
High point: 2150 meters (7054 ft)
Hiking time: 2 days
Backpack

A basic description of the Twin Lakes Loop goes something like this: Hike up Bauerman Valley to a couple of lakes, then go over a low pass and descend Blakiston Valley back to the start. If that description fails to spark your imagination, complete the picture with views, meadows, lakes, waterfalls, a few mountain goats, and a couple of bighorn sheep.

Access: Drive up the Red Rock Parkway 14.6 km to its end (elevation 1500 meters). **(See map on page 187.)**

The Hike: Begin your loop by walking across Red Rock Canyon. On the far side of the bridge, the trail divides. To the left is the Blakiston Creek Trail, which you will follow on the return leg of the loop. For now, go straight and head up the Bauerman Creek Trail. After 50 meters, the pavement ends and the trail continues on an old, abandoned fire road.

Bauerman Valley is forested, with occasional open meadows and avalanche slopes where there are views of the surrounding mountains and ridges. Three creeks must be forded. Only in early

Blakiston Falls

summer is this a problem; generally by midsummer the creeks can be hopped with relative ease.

At 3.9 km the Goat Lake Trail (see trip 50) takes off to the right. From this point, the road climbs steadily to its end at 8.4 km, where there is a small backcountry campsite, a warden's cabin, a horse corral, and a trail intersection.

Go left, cross Lost Creek, then spend the next 3.2 km climbing gradually, but steadily, to Twin Lakes. Just before reaching Upper Twin Lake, a trail branches off to the right, heading to 2140-meter Sage Pass. Upper Twin Lake (elevation 1985 meters) has a backcountry campsite with a cooking shelter and stove.

The trail heads south, traversing high above Lower Twin Lake, then climbing over a low pass. This is not the high point of the loop; the trail continues to climb for another 0.5 km before descending into Blue Grouse Basin. Shortly after passing a small lake, you reach an intersection, 3.1 km from Twin Lakes.

The loop route goes left and heads down Lone Creek valley, then down Blakiston Creek valley. This section of the hike is in the forest, with only occasional views of rocky summits, 1000 meters above.

The trail widens at 12.7 km from Twin Lakes, and suddenly you are surrounded by people who smell of fresh cologne instead of wood smoke and sweat. The attraction is Blakiston Falls. An elaborate viewing platform provides an overlook of this beautiful landmark.

The final kilometer of the loop is an easy stroll on a broad trail to the base of Red Rock Canyon.

52 Lineham Falls

Round trip: 8.4 km (5.4 mi)
Elevation gain: 425 meters (1394 ft)
High point: 2000 meters (6562 ft)
Hiking time: 3 hours
Day hike

Before you start off, it is important to understand what this trail has and what it has not. This trail does not have a destination; it ends in the middle of a meadow, well below the 100-meter waterfall at the end of the valley. What this trail has are views of a spectacular waterfall in a subalpine basin surrounded by the rocky walls of Mount Lineham, Mount Hawkins, Mount Blakiston, and Ruby Ridge.

Above Lineham Falls are the Lineham Lakes. Many hikers have made the mistake of thinking that the falls trail offers an easy cross-country access to the lakes, but it does not. Scaling the cliffs at the end of the valley requires ropes, climbing hardware, and hard hats. If you plan to climb the cliffs, check in at the warden's office before and after your trip.

Access: From the Waterton townsite, drive up the Akamina Parkway for 9.5 km. Park at an unmarked turnout on the right side of the road (elevation 1575 meters).

The Hike: There is no sign along the road marking the start of the Lineham Falls Trail. Walk into the forest on a well-defined track for 50 meters to find the official trail sign. From this point, the trail climbs. With a single steep switchback, the trail ascends from the forested Cameron Creek valley to open meadows above Lineham Creek.

At the end of 1.9 km the trail reenters the forest and the climb slackens. A narrow gorge through an old moraine at 3.8 km marks the entrance into Lineham Creek basin.

A small sign in a meadow at 4.2 km marks the end of the maintained trail. The two trails that continue on head to the cliffs and the climbing routes up to Lineham Lakes. Hikers who would like to continue up the valley to the base of the falls may follow either of

Lineham Falls

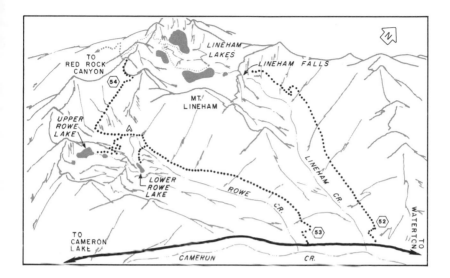

the boot-beaten paths. When the chosen trail begins to climb steeply towards the cliff, leave it and scramble over the talus, up the valley to the falls.

53 Rowe Lakes

Round trip· 12 km (7.5 mi)
Elevation gain: 410 meters (1345 ft)
High point: 2010 meters (6594 ft)
Hiking time: 5 hours
Day hike or backpack

Like diamonds, these two lakes appear slightly different every time you look at them. In the early summer the lakes lie in a setting of brilliant flowers, dominated by the white tassels of bear grass. In midsummer, the lakes take on a greenish glow, reflecting the color of the surrounding hillsides. By autumn the surrounding huckleberry fields and tamarack trees tint the water a shimmering golden yellow.

Access: From the Waterton townsite, drive to the eastern edge of town, then head up the Akamina Parkway for 10.6 km to the

Upper Rowe Lake and Mount Rowe

Rowe Lakes–Tamarack trailhead (elevation 1600 meters). **(See map on page 193.)**

The Hike: The trail begins with a steep climb up a forested hillside. The trail brushes close to Rowe Creek at several points, popular stops for hikers who need to catch their breath before continuing.

After the first kilometer the climb slackens and the trail heads up the Rowe Creek valley, first through forest, then across meadows. The first junction is reached at 3.5 km. The trail on the left heads 0.5 km across the valley to Lower Rowe Lake, located at the base of a cliff. The upper lake is at the top of that cliff, 235 meters above.

The main trail continues for another 1.2 km to Rowe Meadow at the end of the valley. A backcountry campground, the closest camp area to the Rowe Lakes, is located here.

The trail traverses the meadow, crosses a creek, then divides. Go left and climb steeply up a slope. The several well-used spur trails passed along the way are actually animal paths made by the bighorn sheep and mountain goats that inhabit the cliffs above the meadow.

At 6 km the trail reaches Upper Rowe Lake (elevation 2010 meters). A gravel shore invites hikers to linger and ponder the drifting clouds, while meadows beckon the feet to wander among the tamaracks to the base of Mount Rowe.

54 Lineham Ridge and Lineham Lakes

Round trip to Lineham Ridge: 16.2 km (10.1 mi)
Elevation gain: 970 meters (3182 ft)
High point: 2570 meters (8432 ft)
Hiking time: 6 hours
Day hike or backpack

Round trip to Lineham Lakes: 19.6 km (12.3 mi)
Elevation gain: 1020 meters in (3346 ft); 350 meters out (1148 ft)
High point: 2570 meters (8432 ft)
Hiking time: 2 days
Backpack

A windswept ridge with an incredible view and four secluded lakes are the rewards for completing this difficult hike. The trail is steep and rough. The final section to the ridge crest is more like a rock scramble than a trail. Hikers should come prepared with good shoes for the steep pitches and a jacket for protection from the wind at the top.

From Lineham Ridge it's an easy cross-country hike to the beautiful Lineham Lakes basin. Although there is no official trail, hiking boots have beaten an easy-to-follow path down the scree slope to the lakes. Although there is no official backcountry campsite at the lakes, primitive camping is permitted. Be sure to obtain a permit and a list of regulations before you head out.

Access: From the Waterton townsite, drive up the Akamina Parkway for 10.6 km to the Rowe Lakes–Tamarack trailhead (elevation 1600 meters). **(See map on page 193.)**

The Hike: The broad and well-graded trail begins by climbing out of the Cameron Creek valley into the narrow Rowe Creek valley. Meadows alternate with bands of trees until the trail reaches Rowe Meadow and the backcountry campsite at 5.1 km.

The trail crosses the meadow and divides at the far side. The left fork climbs to Upper Rowe Lake (see trip 53 for details). Go right on the Tamarack Trail and head nearly straight up the steep hillside. After 0.5 km of a muscle-wrenching climb, the trail sets off on a steeply ascending traverse over open talus slopes. Near the top, orange markers have been placed along the route to keep you from straying in low-light conditions.

Trail to Lineham Lakes after August snowstorm

The trail climbs to a well-defined saddle, then turns west to follow the ridge, away from Mount Lineham, to an unnamed crest. The narrow trail nearly disappears near the top. Acrophobes will need plenty of help or should skip the final 10 meters, where the trail sends you scrambling up bands of rock and over loose talus to the 2570-meter high point.

The Tamarack Trail continues on all the way to Red Rock Canyon; however, if Lineham Lakes are your goal, leave the trail and follow the ridge line down to a saddle, then uphill toward Mount Hawkins. When you have regained about the same amount of elevation you dropped to reach the saddle, start looking for the cairn that marks the descent to Lineham Lakes. If the trail down looks difficult, you have found the wrong one and should go back and try again. The correct path stays on the talus and avoids the cliffs as it descends to the lakes.

55 Carthew–Alderson Traverse

One way: 19 km (11.8 mi)
Elevation gain: 700 meters (2297 ft)
High point: 2360 meters (7743 ft)
Hiking time: 7 hours
Day hike or backpack

This very popular traverse from Cameron Lake to the Waterton townsite is an ideal one-way hike. Moderately difficult, it takes you to high alpine country at windswept Carthew Pass, then descends along the shores of high alpine lakes, across beautiful meadows, past waterfalls, and through deep cirques on the way back to the townsite.

The traverse is usually hiked in one day. However, if you would like to linger along the route, there is a backcountry camp area at Alderson Lake.

Access: Transportation is not a problem, even if you don't have two vehicles at your disposal. A hiker's shuttle bus departs every morning from Tamarack Mall; check with the Visitor Information Centre or at the sports shop in the mall for departure times. If you are traveling on a tight budget, make your way to the start of the Akamina Parkway and use your ingenuity to get a ride to the road's end at Cameron Lake (elevation 1660 meters).

The Hike: Walk past the boat rental office and go left around the end of the lake. Shortly after crossing the outlet, the trail begins to climb the forested hillside with well-graded switchbacks. The

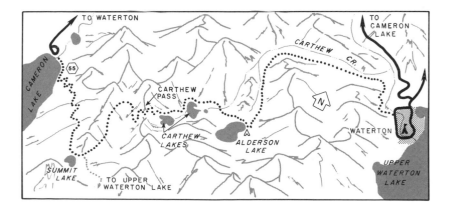

Hikers at crest of Carthew Pass

gradual climb ends in 3.6 km at Summit Lake (elevation 1930 meters). With a horizon line fringed with ragged summits, this lake would be a delightful destination, if there wasn't so much better ahead.

At Summit Lake the trail divides. The Carthew–Alderson Trail goes to the left, climbing for the next 3.6 km to talus-strewn Carthew Pass, the 2360-meter high point of the hike. Views from the pass are superb. To the south lies a veritable wall of mountains with two large lakes at the base, Nooney and Wurdeman.

The trail descends on loose talus toward the three Carthew Lakes. There may be a few moments of confusion, as trails branch out in every direction. Try to stay on the main trail and avoid creating yet another path in the soft soil.

Wind around the shore of the upper lake, then descend, in a couple of easy switchbacks, to the middle lake. At this point the trail hops over rocks on the lakeshore, then drops out of the lake basin, into a subalpine valley. Watch for bears: the next section of the hike passes through an area favored by the local grizzly bear population.

A series of switchbacks brings hikers down into a walled cirque, skirting the monstrous crescent-shaped rock wall to reach Alderson Lake at the base, 11.7 km from the trailhead. The backcountry campsite, a picnic shelter, and an outhouse are located a short distance off the main trail on the lakeshore.

The final 7.3 km are spent hiking in a forested valley. Just when the forest becomes monotonous, the Akamina Parkway appears on the left and, 0.8 km beyond, Waterton Lake and the townsite come into view.

The final leg of the hike is a rapid descent along Cameron Falls. Near the bottom, the trail divides. Stay left and descend to the end of the trail at the base of the falls.

56 Forum Lake and Wall Lake

Round trip to Forum Lake: 9.4 km (5.9 mi)
Elevation gain: 335 meters (1099 ft)
High point: 2010 meters (6594 ft)
Hiking time: 4 hours
Day hike

Round trip to Wall Lake: 11.4 km (7.1 mi)
Elevation gain: 115 meters (377 ft)
High point: 1790 meters (5873 ft)
Hiking time: 4 hours
Day hike or backpack

Two small lakes, just west of the Waterton Lakes National Park boundary, lure hikers out of the park and across the Continental Divide to the Akamina–Kishinena Provincial Recreation Area of British Columbia. Although these two lakes are not in the national park, they are in no sense second-rate. Wall and Forum lakes rank

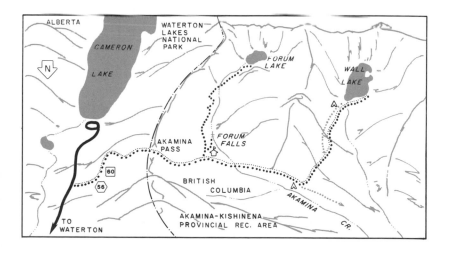

Forum Lake after summer snowstorm

among the best in this area: delicate lakes in subalpine settings, nearly overshadowed by towering cliffs.

No camping is allowed in the fragile environment around Forum Lake. However, there are campsites in the valley along Akamina Creek and at Wall Lake. Be prepared to pay for a campsite. An "Iron Ranger" (a pole with a slot in it) waits along the trail to collect a healthy fee from backpackers.

Access: From the east end of the Waterton townsite, drive up the Akamina Parkway for 14.5 km to the Akamina Pass trailhead (elevation 1675 meters).

The Hike: The trail follows an old road, built in the 1890s. It climbs steeply up the forested hillside for 1.6 km to Akamina Pass (elevation 1790 meters), which is on the Continental Divide, the border of Waterton Lakes National Park, and the provincial boundary between Alberta and British Columbia.

Beyond the pass, the trail descends for 1 km to an intersection; Forum Lake and the park headquarters are to the left, Wall Lake is straight ahead.

To go to Forum Lake, head left. At 0.3 km a short spur trail branches right to a deep grotto and Forum Falls. The lake trail heads nearly straight up the steep hillside, gaining maximum elevation with the least amount of trail. The climb doesn't last long, and 1.8 km from the ranger station, the trail ends at Forum Lake.

To go to Wall Lake, from the Forum Lake intersection, continue to follow the old road along Akamina Creek for another 0.5 km. At the base of a short descent is an intersection. To the right is a camp area; to the left is the trail to Wall Lake.

The Wall Lake Trail contours along the forested hillside for 0.3 km, then divides. The hikers' trail goes uphill, then contours over to Wall Lake. The horse packers' trail remains almost level. Take your pick.

The first campsite is reached 2.1 km from the Forum Lake intersection. This is the hikers' camp area. The horse packers use the camp on the opposite side of the lake.

A high route connects Wall and Forum lakes along the crest of Akamina Ridge. This route should be attempted only by experienced hikers armed with map and compass.

Bicycling

57 Wishbone (Bosporus) Trail

Round trip: 21 km (13 mi)
Elevation gain: 120 meters (394 ft)
High point: 1400 meters (4593 ft)
Riding time: 4 hours
Surface: double and single track dirt
Rating: difficult

Grab a wishbone, squeeze tight, and imagine the perfect bike route: over gently rolling terrain, with large, enchanting meadows, stupendous mountain scenery, and so much wildlife that the route can be lost under their meandering trails. Congratulations! You ended up with the big half of the wishbone, and your wish will come true.

The Wishbone Trail (formally called the Bosporus Trail) is an old stock route that is now open to cyclists. The maintenance on this trail cannot keep up with the rapid growth of brush in this verdant area, and the grassy meadows and forests are frequently very wet after a rainstorm or in the morning. Shoe gaiters are recommended if you want to keep your feet dry. This is a high bear-use area, so make lots of noise as you travel through the brush.

Access: Drive the Chief Mountain International Highway south from its junction with Highway 5. After 500 meters look for a gravel turnout on the left. Park here; the trail begins on the other side of the road.

Log:

0.0 km   The trail starts out on an old wagon that winds its way through groves of birch and aspen and grassy meadows. Views of the surrounding mountains are excellent. In the fall, your chances of hearing the bugling call of a bull elk are better than good. Your chances of seeing a bull and his harem depend on luck. Ride cautiously and make plenty of noise on the trail. Slow down and check for wildlife before entering any meadow.

3.0 km   The route drops down to a large, open meadow just above Lower Waterton Lake. This is the end of the easy riding. The trail now turns into a single track and heads southeast, away from the lake. In some of the wetter areas the trail rut is so deep that it is hard to turn the pedals.

5.0 km   Cross Sofa Creek and head toward Middle Waterton Lake.

6.3 km   Reach a junction with the Vimy Peak Trail. The route up Vimy Peak is for foot and hoof traffic only, so continue straight. The Wishbone Trail narrows as it skirts the edge of Middle Waterton Lake, and the tread becomes rough as it heads over a series of small ridges.

10.5 km   Arrive at Wishbone Landing Backcountry Campground. No bikes are allowed beyond this point. You can park

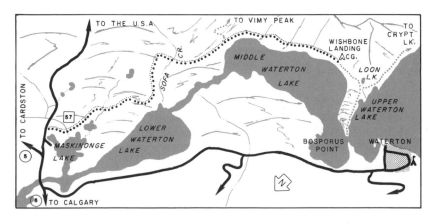

Riding through meadows on Wishbone Trail

your steel (or aluminum) steed here and continue on by foot all the way to Crypt Lake. If you prefer a short jaunt, just to stretch your legs, wander over to Loon Lake or out to Bosporus Point, where saddle horses and their riders swim the narrow channel.

58 Crandell Lake Loop

Loop ride: 21.7 km (13.6 mi)
Elevation gain: 346 meters (1135 ft)
High point: 1625 meters (5331 ft)
Riding time: 6 hours
Surface: paved road and dirt single track
Rating: difficult

This is the premier and most technical of all the mountain bike rides in Waterton–Glacier International Peace Park. Steep, rocky climbs, precipitous ridges, brake-squealing descents, and tire-grinding corners all add up to a day of high-class two-wheeling fun. In the middle of all this riding euphoria are outstanding views of the Blakiston Valley, Cameron Valley, and Middle and Upper Waterton lakes.

Access: Begin your ride at the Information Centre, located 0.6 km east of the Waterton townsite, opposite the entrance to the Prince of Wales Hotel.

Log:

0.0 km   From the Information Centre, cycle the main park road northeast, away from the Waterton townsite. There is no shoulder, and traffic volume is heavy throughout most of the day.

2.9 km   Cross Blakiston Creek and turn left on the Red Rock Canyon Parkway. At this point you must choose between the paved road, which is narrow and usually very busy, or the horse trail, which is narrow and so deeply rutted that, in several sections, it is impossible to turn the pedals. If you choose the horse trail, look for it on the left side of the road at the beginning of the first climb. The following log notations are for the road.

3.4 km   Reach a viewpoint, located on the left side of the road. A short trail leads to an exhibit describing the geological

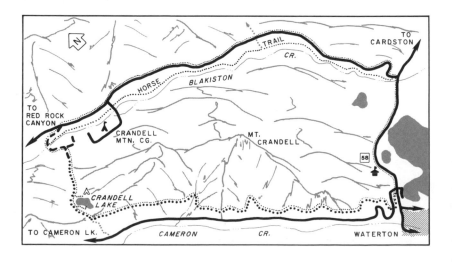

View over Waterton Park townsite from Crandell Lake Trail

and human history of the area. There is also a mountain finder that helps put names to all the peaks you've been admiring. From this point, the road rolls over open prairie, gradually gaining elevation.

4.2 km   A geology exhibit on the right side of the road explains glacial moraines.

5.0 km   A beaver pond exhibit is on the left.

8.0 km   An exhibit on the left explains prehistoric man's activities around the park. The horse trail crosses the exhibit area and can be picked up at this point; however, there are still deep ruts ahead.

9.4 km   An exhibit on the right tells the story of the 1858 Thomas Blakiston Expedition.

9.8 km   Campground access is on the left.

10.9 km   Coppermine Creek Picnic Area is on the right, with picnic tables and rest rooms.

11.1 km   Turn left on a road signed to Canyon Camp and the Crandell Lake trailhead. This is a well-graded gravel road.

11.6 km   Cross Blakiston Creek. The horse trail ends here.

11.8 km   The road divides; take the right fork.

12 km   The Crandell Lake trailhead marks the start of the real fun. For the next 2 km the trail climbs to Crandell Lake. There are numerous challenges: steep ascents, lumpy rocks, and a constant stream of hikers, including young children.

13.9 km   Pass the turnoff to Crandell Lake on the left. The trail leads to the backcountry camp area and picnic shelter. The shore is delicate, so leave the bikes and walk if you wish to visit the lake. The main trail skirts the lake, staying in the forest.

14.2 km   This is the second and last lake access trail. The loop route continues to climb, heading over a forested divide.

14.6 km   Gain the top of the ridge, the 1625-meter high point of this loop. There is a trail junction here. The right fork descends 0.8 km to the Akamina Parkway. The loop route described here takes the left fork and follows the horse trail down the valley.

15 km   Views. The trail is narrow here, so come to a complete stop before checking out the scenery.

17.6 km   The trail descends abruptly to cross a bridge over a small creek, then climbs. This marks the beginning of an up-and-down process that continues for several kilometers. Many of the drops coincide with rocky corners. Use caution. If there are horses on the trail, dismount and allow them to pass before continuing.

18.6 km   View of Upper Waterton Lake.

20.6 km   Cross the Akamina Parkway and descend to a junction. Go left, passing the backyards of several homes.

21.4 km   The trail ends. Go left, uphill, on the main road.

21.7 km   The loop ends at Info Central. Wow! Let's go around again.

59 Bauerman Creek Valley (Snowshoe Trail)

Round trip: 16.4 km (10.3 mi)
Elevation gain: 240 meters (787 ft)
High point: 1740 meters (5709 ft)
Riding time: 2.5 hours
Surface: dirt and gravel road
Difficulty: moderate

Towering peaks and massive rock walls form a spectacular backdrop for this ride on the Snowshoe Trail up the Bauerman Creek valley.

This is not a difficult ride: an old road provides a solid surface the entire distance. However, there are no bridges, and three of the creeks must be forded. Early-season riders may get their feet very wet. By midsummer the creeks may be ridden or hopped, and the ride is fun for all.

Access: Drive, or ride, the Red Rock Parkway 14.7 km to its end. **(See map on page 187.)** The parking lot (elevation 1500 meters) is a popular loitering area for mountain sheep. They hang around, begging for handouts and looking for trash dropped from cars. Please do not feed the sheep and encourage these unhealthy habits.

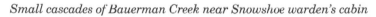

Small cascades of Bauerman Creek near Snowshoe warden's cabin

Paved start of trail through Bauerman Creek valley

Log:

0.0 km   Begin the trip by riding around an interesting geological and cultural display, then head across Red Rock Canyon. At the end of the bridge, the trail divides. The left fork, to the Blakiston Creek valley, is closed to bicycles. Continue straight ahead. After 50 meters the pavement ends, and the trail continues on an old gravel road.

The trail starts in the forest, then climbs up a dry hillside before descending to open meadows on the valley floor. This first section sets the tone for the ride, which has a lot of short climbs and short descents.

4.5 km   Reach an intersection with the Goat Lake Trail, which branches off on the right. This trail is closed to bicycles. From this point on, the road climbs. The climb is generally gradual; however, be ready to shift down for a couple of really steep stretches. Below the road, Bauerman Creek heads down the valley with a series of eye-catching cascades. Above the road, look for mountain goats on the ledges at the base of the cliffs.

8.4 km   The road ends at the Snowshoe warden's cabin. There is a small backcountry camp here. Bicycles cannot be ridden beyond this point. However, if you feel like a walk, Twin Lakes is an easy 3.3-km jaunt to the left, and Lost Lake is a 1.8-km stroll to the right.

60 Wall Lake

Round trip: 11 4 km (7.1 mi)
Elevation gain: 115 meters (337 ft)
High point: 1790 meters (5873 ft)
Riding time: 3 hours
Surface: old dirt road and trail
Rating: difficult

Strong legs are required, if you hope to ride the entire first 1.6 km to Akamina Pass. If you can manage the first steep climb, the rest of the ride—to a medium-size lake dwarfed by the rocky hillsides that box it in on three sides—will seem easy by comparison.

Trail near Wall Lake

Access: From the Waterton townsite, ride or drive the Akamina Parkway for 14.6 km to the Akamina Pass trailhead (elevation 1675 meters). **(See map on page 199.)**

Log:

0.0 km   The trail to Akamina Pass is an old, narrow road built in the 1890s for logging and oil. It climbs steeply up the forested hillside to the pass area.

1.6 km   Reach Akamina Pass (elevation 1790 meters). Several things happen here: you cross the Continental Divide, you leave Alberta and enter British Columbia, you cross the Waterton Lakes National Park border and enter the Akamina–Kishinena Provincial Recreation Area, and you start downhill. Watch out for the waterbars on the descent.

2.6 km   Arrive at an intersection; 200 meters to the left are the park headquarters and the hiking trail to Forum Lake. Continue straight on the old road grade.

3.1 km   The road divides. On the right is the Akamina Creek backcountry camp area. Straight ahead, the old road continues on down the valley. Go left on the Wall Lake Trail and begin a long, level traverse into the Wall Creek valley.

3.4 km   The trail divides, one trail for horses and the other for hikers. Cyclists should ride the horse trail.

4.6 km   Ride by the first of two backcountry campsites. This area is for hikers and cyclists. The campsite on the opposite side of the lake is for those on horseback.

4.7 km   Reach Wall Lake (elevation 1770 meters). A rough trail goes on around the lake if you are looking for a challenge.

On the way out, take another look at the old road. With a bit of determination and a good map, you can ride all the way to Polebridge, an idea that kind of stirs the imagination.

Big Prairie near Polebridge

WINTER

Winter is a very beautiful time in Waterton–Glacier International Peace Park. A blanket of snow adds majesty to the towering peaks, softening the sharp outlines of the concessionaires' buildings and creating a touch of magic in the dark, stately forests. The hills and lakes become quiet as the tourists and their noisy automobiles head back to their homes. The seasonal park personnel, park volunteers, and concession staff depart. Even the water stills as the lakes freeze.

For a brief time in September, the few remaining tourists enjoy the roads and trails at their own pace, unhurried by the crowds. Then, sometime in October or maybe November, the snow begins to fall, covering the roads and closing the park.

During the winter season, Waterton Lakes and Glacier national parks are covered with from 2 to 15 feet (0.6 to 4.5 meters) of snow. Temperatures, from mid-November to April, range between minus 30 degrees to plus 30 degrees Fahrenheit (minus 34 degrees to minus 1 degree Celsius). On the average, the greatest snow accumulation and the coldest temperatures occur in January.

Weather during the winter in the Waterton Lakes–Glacier area is very unpredictable. Visitors packing for a winter trip must be prepared for anything from a warm, hard rain to a blinding blizzard. Waterton Lakes is known for its Chinooks, which are warm, dry winds that cause sudden and rapid melting of the snowpack. In general, expect a lot of dull, cloudy days on the wetter west side of the park and strong, freezing winds on the east side of the mountains.

When the snow falls, many of the roads into and through the parks are gated and closed for the winter. The Going-to-the-Sun Road, Camas Road, Inside North Fork Road, Two Medicine Road, Cut Bank Road, and Many Glacier Road in Glacier National Park are closed. In Waterton Lakes National Park, the Red Rock Parkway and the upper section of the Akamina Parkway are closed.

Winter access is also limited around the periphery of the parks. The Chief Mountain International Highway between Highway 89 and Waterton Park is closed from late September to mid-May. Visitors traveling between the two parks during the winter must drive through Cardston, keeping in mind that the border crossing is only open from 9:00 A.M. to 6:00 P.M. In Montana, there is a winter closure of Highway 49 between East Glacier Park and Highway 89. Visitors traveling between the south and east sides of Glacier National Park must detour east to Browning. Travel to Polebridge on

Bighorn sheep

the west side of the park is limited to one road, Highway 486 from Columbia Falls.

When traveling around the parks in the winter, remember that storms can make driving hazardous at any time. If you are not prepared for driving on snow and ice, leave your car at home.

Accommodations And Services

Lodging is very limited during the winter months. West Glacier, Essex, East Glacier Park, Polebridge, and the Waterton townsite have winter accommodations. These are private enterprises, not park concessionaires. For information about winter activities and lodging at Glacier National Park, write to the Superintendent, Glacier National Park, West Glacier, MT 59936. For information on winter facilities in Waterton Lakes National Park, contact Alberta Tourism at their toll-free number (800) 661-1222, or write to the Waterton Chamber of Commerce, Waterton Park, AB T0K 2M0.

Winter camping is allowed at the Apgar Picnic Area and St. Mary Campground in Glacier National Park and at the Pass Creek

Izaak Walton Inn in Essex

Picnic Area in Waterton Lakes. These three areas have limited facilities in the winter: pit toilets and no running water. At Apgar, water is available at the rest rooms in the visitor center. In Waterton, collect your day's supply of water at the Fire Hall.

Activities

The main winter activities in the parks are skiing, snowshoeing, wildlife viewing, and photography. The ski trails and snowshoe routes listed in the following pages are in their best condition from mid-December through the end of February. A brochure, *Ski Trails of Glacier National Park,* is readily available throughout the park or may be obtained by writing to the Park Headquarters, Glacier National Park, West Glacier, MT 59936. The Waterton winter brochure is available by writing to the Superintendent, Waterton Lakes National Park, Waterton Park, AB T0K 2M0. Skiers in Glacier National Park should have touring or backcountry skis. In Waterton Lakes or at Essex, track skis are adequate.

Wildlife viewing and photography are rewarding activities during the winter. The animals, driven out of the high country by snow and bad weather, spend winter in the sheltered valley bottoms. Areas such as Polebridge, St. Mary, and the Waterton townsite are well known for winter wildlife viewing.

Due to the high risk of avalanches in the parks during most of the winter, mountain climbing and backcountry skiing are not common activities. If you plan to climb or ski into the interior of the park, you must register before starting out.

All overnight trips into the parks must be registered with a park ranger or warden. There are some special winter rules: no wood fires, no pets on snow-covered trails or roadways, no camping more than two nights in one spot, and all overnighting must be done at least 100 feet (30 meters) away from roadways, trails, creeks, or lakes.

Bears

Believe it or not, bears can be a problem, even during their winter hibernation period. Bears may wake up for short periods of time, especially if the weather has been warmer than normal. When camping, use the normal precautions: cook away from the tent, do not sleep in the clothes you cooked in, and be sure to hang your food and garbage.

Winter Ratings

Winter trips are rated as easy, moderate, or difficult. These categories were designed with the cross-country skier in mind; however, snowshoers and hikers may also find them useful.

Easy. Trips in this category are on wide roads with little elevation gain. Even first-time skiers will enjoy these outings.

Moderate. This category includes trips that require some skill. Skiers may encounter steep hills that will be difficult to negotiate when icy.

Difficult. This category involves trails that were intended for summer hiking use. Specially designed "backcountry" skis and heavy "backcountry" boots are recommended. Previous skiing experience is a requirement.

WEST GLACIER

Facilities

Of all the areas open to visitors in Glacier National Park during the winter months, West Glacier is the most popular. The Amtrak depot (West Glacier Station) is a common pickup spot for hotel and

Winter visitors should dress in layers.

lodge guests from the entire area. Tourist facilities in town are limited to the Highland Motel, a few rental cars (Rent-a-Wreck), a restaurant, and a small grocery store. However, West Glacier is close to several larger population centers where lodging is readily available, such as Coram, Columbia Falls, Whitefish, and Kalispell.

The headquarters for Glacier National Park is located in West Glacier, and Park Service personnel are available on weekdays to answer questions about road conditions or avalanche hazards, issue backcountry use permits, and sell maps. On weekends the Apgar Visitor Center, near the shores of Lake McDonald, is open with all the same services. For "front country" campers, the Apgar Picnic Area on the lakeshore is open for overnighting. Facilities include an outhouse, picnic tables, and fire grates (bring your own firewood). Water is available from the open rest room at the visitor center.

Whether you have come just to enjoy the scenery or for strenuous winter recreation, West Glacier is an ideal place to visit the park. The views up Lake McDonald to the Garden Wall are excellent. The road around the lake is plowed for most of the winter, allowing visitors access to more tremendous views. For skiers and snowshoers there are marked trails starting from the Apgar Visitor Center, and the unplowed roads allow for longer tours on the Going-to-the-Sun, Camas, and Inside North Fork roads.

Winter Tours

61 Going-To-The-Sun Road

Round trip to Avalanche Campground: 8 miles (12.8 km)
Elevation gain: 200 feet (61 m)
High point: 3400 feet (1036 m)
Rated: easy

At the upper end of Lake McDonald there is a delightful opportunity to discover the magic of winter while touring the lower portion of the Going-to-the-Sun Road. This is a quiet place after the snow falls, and visitors may take their time while exploring the wonders of the upper McDonald Creek valley. On clear days, snow-plastered summits and the awe-inspiring Garden Wall dominate the skyline. On cloudy days, groves of western red cedar and icy cascades on upper McDonald Creek vie for attention.

Access: Drive the Going-to-the-Sun Road 12.5 miles, from West Glacier toward Logan Pass. Park at the end of the plowed road (elevation 3200 feet).

The Tour: The road divides at the parking area; the Going-to-the-Sun Road continues straight ahead. Walk past the ski hut (a small open shelter with information), head around the gate, then start up the road.

The tour begins with a gradual climb through the forest. McDonald Falls is passed at 0.2 mile and can be seen from the left side of the road. The gradual climb continues until the road reaches the Sacred Dancing Cascade Overlook (the name says it all) at 0.8

Going-to-the-Sun Road is ideal for beginning skiers.

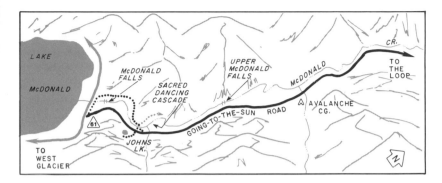

mile. The cascade may be seen from the road or by descending a short, skiable trail to a bridge.

The road levels a bit, passing several small beaver ponds, then begins to climb again just before reaching the Upper McDonald Creek Falls Viewing Platform at 2.1 miles. The platform overlooks a narrow gorge and cascading McDonald Creek. Take off your skis and walk down the stairs to the platform.

The road levels again as it passes through a narrow section of the valley. Views are fascinating as the road skirts the edge of the creek between the towering walls of Mount Brown and Mount Vaught. When the valley widens again, the road moves away from the creek and heads through the forest until it reaches the Avalanche Campground and Picnic Area at 4 miles. This is a good place to have lunch before heading back down the valley.

When the snowpack is stable, it is possible to continue on up the Going-to-the-Sun Road all the way to The Loop, located at 12.1 miles from the parking area. The Loop lies at the base of the Garden Wall, at the edge of an extremely hazardous avalanche zone.

62 McGee Meadow Loop

Loop trip: 12 miles (19.2 km)
Elevation gain: 767 feet (234 m)
High point: 3900 feet (1189 m)
Rated: moderate

This is a true winter adventure, with snow-covered meadows, forests, and mountain scenery. Along the way, search for the tracks of rabbits, deer, coyotes, and mountain lions. Overhead, watch for geese cruising to and from the open waters of Lake McDonald.

Access: The loop trip begins on the north side of lower McDonald Creek. Turn off Highway 2 at West Glacier and drive 2.1 miles into the park. At a T intersection, turn left onto the Camas Road and drive 0.6 mile to a gate. Park here (elevation 3173 feet).

The Tour: Head up the Camas Road, following the signs to Polebridge. At 0.7 mile the road to Fish Creek Campground branches off on the right; this will be the return route. For now, continue straight.

The road climbs steadily, with occasional views of the surrounding summits. This is an easy climb, except when the trail is unbroken after a new snowfall.

Leave the Camas Road when it reaches the McGee Meadow Overlook at 5.2 miles, and ski out into the meadow. Bear left and follow the trees around the northern end of the open area. At the northeast corner of the meadow a series of orange markers has been

Skier at McGee Meadow

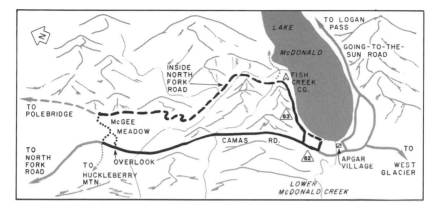

set in the snow to guide you into a dense lodgepole pine forest. The route tunnels through the forest on a wide trail. However, snowdrifts and rolling terrain make this short section the most difficult of the tour.

The trail ends at the Inside North Fork Road. Go right on the narrow road and climb for 0.5 mile to the crest of a ridge before descending along a steep hillside. A few sections of the road can be difficult when icy, but for the most part it is easy going. The descent ends at Fish Creek Campground, at 10.2 miles.

From the campground, head to the right, following the road along the shores of Lake McDonald for a pleasant and scenic 0.5 mile. When the road leaves the lakeshore there is a steep 0.6-mile climb back to the Camas Road. The loop trip ends with a well-earned glide back down the Camas Road to the gate.

63 Fish Creek Campground

Loop trip: 3.4 miles (5.4 km)
Elevation gain: 200 feet (61 m)
High point: 3350 feet (1021 m)
Rated: easy

This is a short, fun, and very scenic loop along the edge of Lake McDonald. On a clear day the views are panoramic, covering an endless array of snow-covered summits from the Belton Hills to the Continental Divide.

Skiing along shore of Lake McDonald

Access: Drive to the Camas Road gate (see trip 62). **(See map on page 221.)**

The Tour: Begin by heading up the Camas Road, climbing steadily for 0.7 mile to an intersection. Go right, following the sign to the Fish Creek Campground, and swoosh downhill for 0.6 mile to the lakeshore. Another 0.4 mile of easy skiing takes you to the campground and picnic area. Eat your lunch at the picnic area on the lakeshore, then zip around the campground loops before heading back down the lake.

To make the loop, ski back along the lakeshore. When the road begins to climb up to the Camas Road, look for an overgrown road branching off on the left. This intersection is unmarked, so you must look carefully to find it. The road you are looking for is a narrow, old forest road that passes several private cabins, then descends in a rush to a plowed road paralleling Lower McDonald Creek. Follow the road to the right for a couple hundred feet to return to the Camas Road gate.

POLEBRIDGE

Facilities

Difficult access and limited facilities make Polebridge the least-used winter area of Glacier National Park. However, if you're looking for a scenic place to ski or snowshoe away from the crowds, the west side of the park is it. Polebridge is also an ideal area for spotting wildlife. A large population of white-tailed deer lives in the valley, as well as mule deer and elk. Ski trails are generally crisscrossed with their tracks, in addition to those of coyotes and an occasional mink or beaver.

To reach Polebridge in the winter, drive Highway 2 for 13 miles north from Kalispell or 16 miles southwest from West Glacier to the small town of Columbia Falls. Head north on Highway 486. The first 12.6 miles of the drive are on pavement; the last 23.8 miles are on a mostly dirt road. Road conditions may be bad. Compact snow and ice, deep ruts, and endless potholes are the norm.

(Note: This road receives only intermittent plowing, which means the road has a low priority rating and will not be plowed immediately after a heavy snowfall. Always carry a shovel and tire chains.)

Visitor services in Polebridge include a small general store and a hostel. The store has limited winter hours, so don't plan any last-minute shopping there. The hostel is excellent. It has bunk rooms, semiprivate rooms, a couple of small cabins, and a large cabin that may be rented on a weekly basis. The hostel offers a shower, a living room, and a communal kitchen. Ski rentals are available. Transportation may be arranged from the Amtrak station in West Glacier. Rates are cheap. For information, write to the North Fork Hostel, Box 1, Polebridge, MT 59928, or phone (406) 888-5241.

For skiing or snowshoeing, drive through the town of Polebridge and cross the North Fork Flathead River to the park entrance and ranger station. The road is gated beyond this point. From the parking area you can head out in three directions on park roads. The two most popular destinations are Big Prairie and Bowman Lake (see trips 64 and 65). If you have any questions or need a backcountry use permit, contact the ranger on duty by wandering through the compound or calling from the courtesy phone at the entrance station.

Winter Tours

64 Big Prairie

Round trip: 5 miles (8 km)
Elevation gain: none
High point: 3600 feet (1097 m)
Rated: easy

Nestled between the North Fork Flathead River and a rugged wall of snow-covered peaks lies the 4.5-mile-long and 1-mile-wide expanse of Big Prairie. The nearly level approach, on the unplowed Inside North Fork Road, is easy, and the prairie is a delight for skiers, who can take off in any direction, creating their own trails or skating courses. The open prairie is an excellent place for a winter campsite and perfect for moonlight ski tours.

Access: Drive to the Polebridge Entrance (see the Polebridge Facilities section for directions) and park in the area provided (elevation 3600 feet).

The Tour: Head uphill, past the gate, to the intersection with

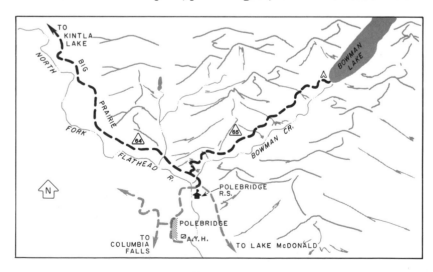

Skier near Big Prairie

the Inside North Fork Road. Head left (north), and descend to and cross Bowman Creek to a second intersection. Stay left, on the valley floor, paralleling the North Fork Flathead River.

The 1988 Red Bench Fire burnt off most of the timber on the valley floor, so the views are excellent. To the east, at the heart of Glacier National Park, the rugged peaks of the Continental Divide can be seen. To the west, the rolling snow-covered hills of the Flathead National Forest are visible. The new crop of aspens and lodgepole pines are growing rapidly, but the feeling of openness should remain for many years.

Several minor prairies are passed along the way. However, when Big Prairie is reached at 2.0 miles, it is unmistakable: wide-open expanses with small stands of trees that escaped the fire. The several rustic log cabins that dot the prairie are reminders that before the park was formed, ranching was popular in the North Fork Flathead River valley. The park has bought out the two largest ranches, the MC and the Quarter Moon; however, a couple of the smaller holdings are still privately owned. The park will buy out the rest when the opportunity arises.

"Camp robber" (gray jay) is a real winter scavenger

The prairie continues for 4.5 miles, then ends at the base of a forested hill. The road continues on, reaching Round Prairie at 7.7 miles from Polebridge and ending at the Kintla Lake Campground in 14.7 miles. The entire tour to Kintla Lake is easy, with only 1 mile of steady climbing near the end.

65 Bowman Lake

Round trip: 12 miles (19 km)
Elevation gain: 470 feet (144 m)
High point: 4070 feet (1241 m)
Rated: moderate

In a narrow, glacier-carved valley lies beautiful 7-mile-long Bowman Lake. The lake is an excellent ski tour or snowshoe destination from the Polebridge Ranger Station on an unplowed forest road.

The tour is challenging. The road is steep, and the descents may be hazardous when icy.

Access: Drive to the Polebridge Ranger Station (see the Polebridge Facilities section for directions). **(See map on page 224.)**

The Tour: From the parking area (elevation 3558 feet), ski uphill and pass the gate to reach a T intersection. Go left and head

Ice- and snow-covered Bowman Lake

Kick-turn

north on the Inside North Fork Road. The road descends to cross Bowman Creek, then divides. Take the right fork and head uphill on a steep, winding road. For the first 3 miles the road passes through forest burnt in the 1988 Red Bench Fire. This area is now the home of a large population of white-tailed deer. Watch for the deer on the open slopes or down by the creek as you head up.

At the top of the hill, near the halfway point, the road leaves the burn area, and the remainder of the trip is in the forest. The road descends, then rolls over several steep hills. At 5.5 miles pass a small meadow, then descend for the final 0.5 mile to the lakeshore.

If you are planning to camp, the forested campground offers excellent protection from the winds that race across the lake. An outhouse is left open for winter use. Skiing up the lake is a popular activity; however, before heading out, check with the ranger at Polebridge to determine the quality of the ice. In any case, stay away from the thin ice at the outlet.

ESSEX–IZAAK WALTON INN

Facilities

Essex, location of the Izaak Walton Inn and very little else, is the hub of cross-country skiing in the Glacier National Park area. The management at the inn sets more than 30 km (more than 20 miles) of groomed tracks, some for skating and all for diagonal striders. Telemarkers have a hill for themselves, and backcountry skiers have the north and south Dickey Bowls to explore.

The groomed cross-country ski trails are open to all; however, skiers who are not guests at the inn are required to pay a trail-use

Ice-covered vegetation near small creek

Breaking trail

fee at the reception desk. For skiers who do not wish to pay the fees or ski groomed trails, there are challenging ski tours on the Ole Creek Trail at nearby Walton and on the Autumn Creek Trail at Marias Summit on Highway 2 (see trips 66 and 67).

The town of Essex originated as a work station for the Great Northern Railroad. The Izaak Walton Inn was built to house the thirty or so workers it took to keep the tracks open over Marias Pass throughout the winter and to run the helper engines that gave trains an extra push over the Continental Divide at Marias Pass.

Today, work crews and helper engines are still part of the scene at Essex. And, although the inn is privately owned, the tracks run right by the front door. The inn has retained a railroad feeling, and guests can even choose to stay in a caboose.

The Izaak Walton Inn provides the only services at Essex. These include lodging, food service, ski rentals, groomed ski trails, a laundromat, a sauna, and guided ski trips into Glacier National Park. Visitors can arrive by Amtrak at the Essex depot and stay at the inn or rent a car and tour the park at their leisure. For information, write to the Izaak Walton Inn, P.O. Box 653, Essex, MT 59916, or call (406) 888-5700.

Winter Tours

66 Ole Creek Trail

Round trip: 14 miles (22.4 km)
Elevation gain: 600 feet (183 m)
High point: 4500 feet (1371 m)
Rated: difficult

The Ole Creek Trail is a challenging tour up a narrow valley on the southeast side of the park. The route follows a hiking trail and is ideal for snowshoes. Skiers may have difficulties negotiating some of the narrow and steep sections of trail and should only attempt this tour on heavy-duty backcountry equipment. The trail crosses several avalanche areas, so avalanche beacons, probe poles, and shovels should be part of everyone's equipment.

Access: The trip begins at the Walton Ranger Station, located on Highway 2 at the southeast corner of the park. To get there from Essex, drive east on Highway 2, cross the Middle Fork Flathead

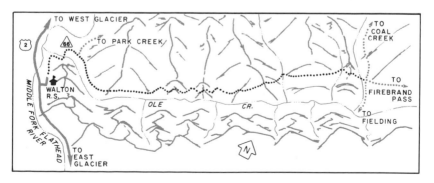

Skier crossing suspension bridge over Ole Creek

River, then take the first left turn to the ranger station, elevation 3720 feet.

The Tour: From the backcountry parking area, the trail starts off with a short, steep climb to the top of a wooded terrace. This is followed by a fun traverse through the forest for 0.5 mile, then a descent to Ole Creek, which is crossed on a suspension bridge.

The 0.5-mile section beyond Ole Creek is the most difficult of the trip. The trail is narrow and often invisible as it climbs steeply across a precipitous hillside above the creek.

At 1 mile cross a wide saddle, then descend to an intersection. Go right and begin a long, nearly level traverse around the base of Scalplock Mountain. The route is poorly marked and, after a heavy snowfall, you must use your imagination on the open, and occasionally avalanche-prone, slopes.

As you head up the valley, views of the Flathead Range, which borders the south side of the park, are excellent. You may also want to watch for the large herd of elk that winters in the Ole Creek drainage. After 2.3 miles the valley opens up a bit, and skiing for the next 4.7 miles is considerably easier. At 7 miles the Fielding Coal Creek Trail is reached. This is an ideal turnaround point.

67 Marias Pass–Autumn Creek Trail

One way: 6 miles (9.6 km)
Elevation loss: 960 feet (293 m)
High point: 5500 feet (1676 m)
Rated: difficult

The most popular winter trip in the Marias Pass area is a one-way ski tour down the southwest side of the pass. This beautiful tour passes frozen lakes, skirts snow-covered trees, and ends with a long, exciting descent. Along the way the route passes several vista points, excellent sun bathing and picnic sites, and open slopes for telemarking. If you can arrange the transportation, this is the tour to make. If not, skiing or snowshoeing around the Marias Pass area to the lakes and the open slopes on the Blacktail Hills is a very agreeable alternative.

Access: Drive Highway 2 to Marias Pass (elevation 5280 feet). If you have two cars, leave one in a small, unmarked turnout on the west side of the pass, 4 miles below the summit at milepost 193.8 (located 1.8 miles above the chain-up area on the eastbound side of the road). Take the second car to the summit and park on the westbound side of the road between the highway and the railroad tracks. If you don't have two cars, you'll have to take your chances hitchhiking or walk the highway back up to the summit.

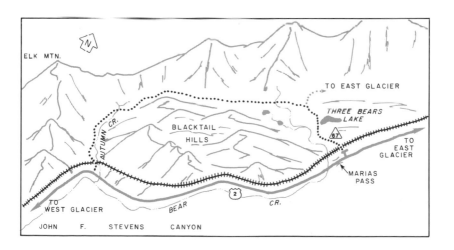

The Tour: Walk across the tracks at the point where three tracks merge into two tracks. After crossing the tracks, go straight to the trees, then head left to find the trailhead. The trail is marked with orange markers or poles throughout; however, these markers are not always easy to find.

Following the Continental Divide Trail, climb gradually through the forest to Three Bears Lake and an intersection at 1 mile. Go left over rolling terrain, heading steadily up to a wide divide (elevation 5440 feet). The trail now descends into the Autumn Creek drainage, tucked in between the Blacktail Hills and Elk Mountain.

At the western end of the Blacktail Hills, the valley bends toward the south and begins to head steadily down into John F. Stevens Canyon. The trail leaves the meadows and enters the forest, where the trees give an added dimension to the excitement of the descent. The terrain continues to steepen, and skis are flying by the time you reach the railroad tracks. However, it is not until you cross the tracks and head down the service road on the opposite side that you have a real chance to break the sound barrier. The road plummets down to Highway 2, where you parked your second car.

Telemarking on Blacktail Hills

EAST GLACIER PARK

Facilities

The town of East Glacier Park, with its huge hotel, numerous motels, and guest cabins, is very quiet during the winter months, when most of these places are closed. Even Highway 49, the shortcut link between East Glacier Park and St. Mary, closes when the snow flies, forcing traffic to make the detour east to Browning.

However, with a little searching, one open motel, Porter's Alpine, can be found just off Highway 2 on a side street. Travelers will also find a gas station, a convenience store, and a restaurant/bar.

There is a ranger station in East Glacier Park, located on Highway 49, which has minimum staffing throughout the winter. The rangers have marked two routes for cross-country skiers. The Midvale Creek Loop begins just north of the Mountain Pine Motel and ends after 4 miles near the Glacier Park Lodge. The second trail is a one-way descent from milepost 203 on Highway 2 near Lubec, ending near the Glacier Park Lodge. The most scenic winter trip is the tour to Two Medicine Lake (see trip 68).

Winter Tours

68 Two Medicine Lake

Round trip: 15.5 miles (24.8 km)
Elevation gain: 233 feet (71 m)
High point: 5164 feet (1574 m)
Rating: easy

This is one of the most beautiful winter tours in the park. The entire trip follows an unplowed road that winds around Lower Two Medicine Lake (a reservoir), then climbs into a narrow valley, flanked by towering peaks, to end at Two Medicine Lake. Views are outstanding from the parking area to the end of the tour.

Access: From the town of East Glacier Park, drive north on

Lower Two Medicine Lake under winter coat of ice

Highway 49. This road is plowed but poorly maintained during the winter months. At 4 miles the road ends at a gated intersection. Park here (elevation 4931 feet).

The Tour: From the Highway 49 gate, two roads branch out on the left. Take the upper of the two, which stays above the dam, and head around the north side of Lower Two Medicine Lake. For the first 3 miles snowmobiles are allowed on the road; however, once the park gate is passed, the road belongs to the quiet winter travelers.

As the road rounds the upper end of the lake, Sinopah Mountain and Mount Helen come into view. The park entrance station is passed at 4 miles, and the road continues its nearly level course up the valley for another 1.5 miles to Two Medicine Creek. Watch on the right side of the road for a wide turnout and a rest room that mark the start of a short and very interesting side trip to Running Eagle Falls. The falls is located 0.2 mile up a side valley. The route follows a wide trail over a nearly level flood plain to the confluence of the Dry Fork and Two Medicine Creek. The falls is to the right and is frequently festooned with icicles.

Continuing on to the lake, the road crosses Two Medicine Creek, then begins a 1.6-mile climb. At 7.1 miles the road crests a forested saddle, then begins to descend. There is an intersection at 7.5 miles where the road divides. To the right lies a picnic area, a campground, and little Pray Lake. To the left, the main road continues on to the shores of Two Medicine Lake.

Do not ski on the lake unless it is well frozen, and always stay on the south side to avoid avalanches. Check ice conditions with a ranger at East Glacier Park before you start out.

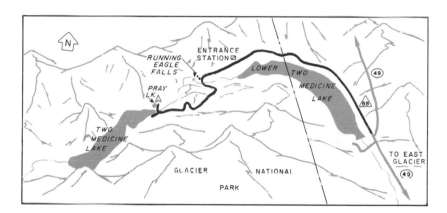

ST. MARY

Facilities

St. Mary is a bustling town during the summer, but during the winter all is quiet. The only noise and activity around the boarded-up inn, gas station, and tourist shops is the howl of the wind as it rushes down the lake and out to the eastern prairies. Camping is permitted at the St. Mary Campground, located 0.3 mile past the park entrance booths. The campground has pit toilets, picnic tables, and fire grates, but no water. There is also a herd of elk in residence throughout most of the winter.

The St. Mary store is open all winter, with groceries and limited camping supplies.

Skiing through forest toward Red Eagle Lake on snowy day

Several winter trails have been marked for skiers near the shore of St. Mary Lake. Three of these trails are loops, which range from 1 mile to 3.5 miles in length. These just-for-fun loops tour around the meadows and forest at the lower end of St. Mary Lake. To find the trails, turn off Highway 89 at the St. Mary winter entrance. Drive for 300 feet, then park at the bulletin board located at the back of the district ranger's office.

The loops are tagged with orange markers, and the intersections are signed. Other tours in the area are the Going-to-the-Sun Road around Red Eagle Lake and St. Mary Lake (trips 69 and 70). For further information, contact the park personnel at the district office during business hours.

In the spring, or when the snow accumulation is low, the road to Many Glacier is opened and skiers and snowshoers have the option of a scenic tour to Grinnell Lake or an equally scenic trip up the Swiftcurrent Valley to Bullhead Lake (see trips 71 and 72). Check with a ranger for current road conditions before heading out.

Winter Tours

69 Red Eagle Lake

Round trip to Red Eagle Creek: 7.6 miles (12.2 km)
Elevation gain: 500 feet (152 m)
High point: 4860 feet (1481 m)
Rated: moderate

Round trip to Red Eagle Lake: 14 miles (22.4 km)
Elevation gain: 366 feet (112 m)
High point: 4860 feet (1481 m)
Rated: difficult

The popular summer hike to Red Eagle Lake makes an excellent winter adventure. The first half of the tour is on an old road that climbs up from the open plains around St. Mary Lake to traverse vast meadows on the hills above. The second half of the tour is on a trail and can be very challenging. The trail crosses Red Eagle Creek twice, without bridges, then works its way up a forested valley to Red Eagle Lake.

Snowshoers will have no trouble in the forest sections of this

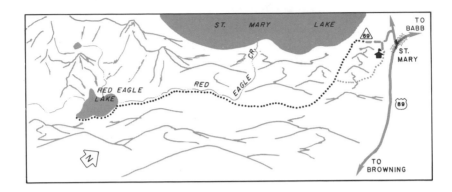

trip; however, skiers going all the way to the lake should have backcountry skis and route-finding ability. Everyone should carry a map and a compass. This tour makes an excellent overnighter, with numerous campsite locations to be found in the meadows, in the forested valley, or near the lake.

Access: Drive Highway 89 to the St. Mary winter entrance. Park at the bulletin board on the north side of the St. Mary Ranger Station (elevation 4541 feet).

The Tour: Follow the ski trail to Old Red Eagle Road. The old road parallels the lakeshore for a short distance before it begins a steady climb through forest. As the road heads up, watch for mountain lion tracks, which are occasionally seen in this area. At 4800 feet the road levels out, then heads southwest through open meadows and past frozen marshes. At 1.5 miles the Elk Loop ski trail comes up through the forest to join the road on the left.

The road continues through alternating bands of trees and broad meadows until it ends at 3.5 miles, at the edge of a bluff overlooking Red Eagle Creek. If you do not intend to ski all the way to the lake, this is an ideal place to turn around.

At this point there are two ways to reach the lake. One way is to follow the summer trail, which drops down the steep slope of the bluff to the creek, crosses the creek, heads up-valley for 1 mile, then recrosses the creek. However, with the bridges removed for the winter, creek crossings are often difficult and dangerous. Unless it is a very cold winter and the creek is frozen solid, it is best to leave the trail at the top of the bluff and head cross-country. To do this, head left and traverse high across the forested hillside for the first 0.5 mile, then gradually descend to the valley floor at about 1 mile. Continue up the valley with the trail.

The final 2.5 miles to the lake are fairly easy going through meadows and forest. The trail stays to the far east side of the valley floor. If you cannot find the trail, simply follow the line of least resistance up the valley to the lakeshore. Do not ski on the lake unless you have checked conditions with a park ranger before heading out.

70 St. Mary Lake

Round trip to Rising Sun: 11 miles (17.6 km)
Elevation gain: none
High point: 4541 feet (1384 m)
Rating: easy

The tour along the edge of St. Mary Lake encompasses the eastern end of the Going-to-the-Sun Road. The unobstructed views and dry, open countryside along the lake provide a fascinating contrast to the lush forest on the west side of the road in the Lake McDonald area.

St. Mary Lake is an easy tour for the whole family.

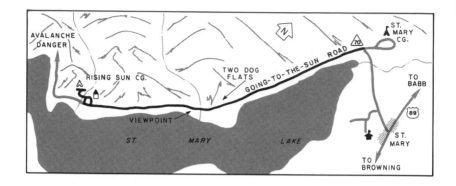

Weather and snow conditions play a major role in this area. Fresh snow is often swept off the open hillsides along the lake by strong winds shortly after it has fallen. The sun warms the hillsides, and the resultant snowmelt may leave patches of exposed road. Check at the ranger station for current conditions before starting out.

Access: Drive Highway 89 to St. Mary and take the winter entrance into the park. Go past the boarded-up visitor center and the park entrance station, then drive on for 0.4 mile to the gate. Park here (elevation 4541 feet).

The Tour: The route up St. Mary Lake is very straightforward: simply follow the snow-covered Going-to-the-Sun Road. The lake is nearly always in sight; however, the views improve after the first mile, when the road begins to traverse the open hillsides. At 2.2 miles pass through an area known as Two Dog Flats, which is a sloping meadow, perfect for practicing a few telemark turns. A mile beyond is a viewpoint of Triple Divide Peak. This unimpressive peak, located at the end of the Hudson Bay Creek drainage, is the dividing point for the three most important drainages in North America. Water descending from the summit of this peak will end up in the Atlantic Ocean, the Pacific Ocean, or Hudson Bay. Water from St. Mary Lake is on its way north to Canada, joining the Saskatchewan River and then the Nelson River before draining into Hudson Bay.

At 5.3 miles the road enters the Rising Sun area. On the right is the Rising Sun Motel and Campground. The tour boat dock is located on the left. This is a good place to turn around and call it a day. A mile beyond the Rising Sun area the road crosses the first of many very active and very dangerous avalanche chutes.

71 Bullhead Lake

Round trip: 5 miles (8 km)
Elevation gain: 320 feet (98 m)
High point: 5200 feet (1585 m)
Rating: moderate

Follow the popular summer trail up the Swiftcurrent Valley, from lake to lake and view to view. At the head of the valley lies Bullhead Lake, in a cathedral-like setting surrounded by the walls of Mount Grinnell, Swiftcurrent Mountain, Mount Wilbur, Mount Henkel, and Altyn Peak.

This trip is not recommended after a heavy snowfall. The sheer walls of the Swiftcurrent Valley descend straight from the ridge crests to the valley floor, creating picture-perfect avalanche slopes.

Access: This is a springtime or low-snow-year trip. Check with the rangers at St. Mary concerning the status of the Many Glacier Road before starting. When the road is open, drive north 9 miles from St. Mary on Highway 89 to Babb. Turn left and head west up the Swiftcurrent Valley for 13 miles to the end of the Many Glacier Road at the Swiftcurrent Motor Inn. Park here (elevation 4880 feet).

The Tour: Follow the Swiftcurrent Trail up-valley from the

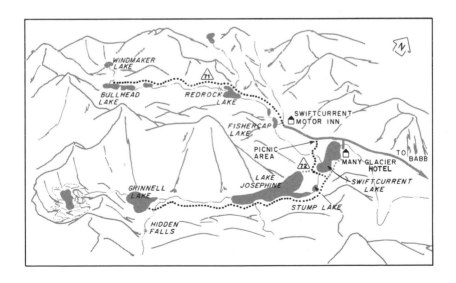

upper end of the parking lot. The trail begins by passing through a dense band of trees, then crossing Wilbur Creek on a log bridge before it begins to climb. The first lake, Fishercap, is passed unseen in the dense aspen and spruce forest. After climbing steadily for 1 mile, the trail turns west and gradually descends to Redrock Lake.

Contour around Redrock Lake, then climb over a steepish rib of red rock, threading between exposed bedrock and Redrock Falls. Once on top the trail heads over a rolling, rocky terrace covered with scrub willow, where it is easy to lose the path. Take the extra time required to keep track of the trail as it provides the easiest path through the willow. A couple of small, unnamed lakes are passed before the valley ends at Bullhead Lake.

If energy permits, consider a side trip to Windmaker Lake in a spur valley to the north. Winter provides a special opportunity to visit this lake, which is popular with the grizzlies during the summer.

Skiing above Redrock Lake

72 Grinnell Lake

Round trip: 6.8 miles (11 km)
Elevation gain: 100 feet (30 m)
High point: 4978 feet (1517 m)
Rating: moderate

This is a tour through majestic forest to three scenic lakes. The route follows hiking trails on nearly level terrain all the way to Grinnell Lake. The major difficulties are route finding through the forest and negotiating around the deep and icy moats that form at the base of the trees.

Access is the greatest challenge. The road from Sherburne Dam to Many Glacier is not plowed during the winter months and isn't opened until spring, after the last heavy snowfall. Check at the ranger station in St. Mary for current road conditions.

Access: Drive 9 miles north from St. Mary on Highway 89 to the town of Babb. Go left, up the Swiftcurrent Valley. At 11.5 miles from the turnoff is the huge Many Glacier Hotel. Continue straight for another 0.7 mile and park at the Grinnell Glacier trailhead (elevation 4880 feet). **(See map on page 243.)**

The Tour: Follow the Grinnell Glacier Trail across the meadow, over Swiftcurrent Creek, and around Swiftcurrent Lake. At 0.7 mile, the trail divides. Go left and continue around the lake. (Do not take the right fork; it leads to dangerous avalanche slopes along the shores of Lake Josephine.)

At the southeast corner of Swiftcurrent Lake, cross Cataract Creek on a wide bridge. At this point the trail goes to the left, but do not follow it. Instead, head to the right, between the river and the trees. In 30 feet, when the river bends, go into the trees, and immediately intersect a trail from the Many Glacier Hotel. Go right and follow this trail up the forested valley past Stump Lake.

When you reach Lake Josephine you may either follow the trail through the trees or, if the ice is still solid, ski along the shore to the upper end of the lake.

At the upper end of Lake Josephine, find the trail that heads back into the trees, paralleling Cataract Creek. At 3 miles the trail crosses the creek for the second time. The wires for the suspension bridge over the creek remain in place all winter, but, unfortunately,

Swiftcurrent Creek

all the slats are removed, so skiers and snowshoers must hunt around for a solid snow bridge to cross.

Once across, return to the bridge, then head straight through the trees to Grinnell Lake.

WATERTON TOWNSITE

Facilities

Waterton Lakes National Park has an active nonmotorized winter sports program. Tracks are groomed and set at the end of each week for beginning and intermediate-level skiers. Advanced skiers have plenty of opportunities for backcountry touring.

The Waterton townsite is the liveliest of all the winter access points to the Waterton–Glacier International Peace Park. The Kilmorey Lodge stays open all winter, offering rooms, a lounge, and a restaurant. The small Pass Creek Picnic Area, opposite the Red Rock Parkway, is designated for winter camping. Facilities there include pit toilets and a cook shelter. Water may be taken from Pass Creek and boiled, and water is available at public rest rooms in the fire hall at the center of town. A small, well-stocked grocery store remains open year-round for last-minute supplies.

Rewaxing skis at trailside

The townsite is scenically located at the edge of Upper Waterton Lake, and winter photography is a popular activity from the path along the lakeshore. Bighorn sheep and deer make the townsite their wintering ground and are a common sight in the picnic areas, along the lake, and in the schoolyard.

Overnight trips in the park require a backcountry permit. These may be obtained in the townsite at the Administration Office or the Warden's Office on weekdays from 8:00 A.M. to 4:00 P.M. On weekends, permits are issued at the warden's office only, from 8:30 A.M. to 9:30 A.M. and from 1:00 P.M. to 2:00 P.M.

Winter Tours

73 Cameron Lake Ski Trail

Round trip from Rowe Creek: 10.5 km (6.5 mi)
Elevation gain: 62 meters (200 ft)
High point: 1675 meters (5495 ft)
Rating: moderate

Round trip from Little Prairie Picnic Shelter: 5.5 km (3.5 mi)
Elevation gain: 36 meters (100 ft)
High point: 1675 meters (5495 ft)
Rating: easy

A beautiful lake nestled beneath the vertical walls of Forum Peak is the extremely scenic destination of this tour. The entire trail is groomed once a week, making the tour relatively easy and lots of fun for skiers of all skill levels.

Access: Drive to the Waterton townsite, then head up the Akamina Parkway for 10.6 km to the Rowe Creek trailhead (elevation 1613 meters). The ski trail from here to the Little Prairie Picnic Shelter is rolling, with several short, steep sections for a bit of challenge.

The alternative starting point is the Little Prairie Picnic Shelter, located 4 km beyond Rowe Creek at the end of the plowed road (elevation 1639 meters).

The Tour: From the picnic shelter there are two options for reaching Cameron Lake: the road or the trail. The road is wide and

Skiing across frozen waters of Cameron Lake

the easier of the two to ski. The trail rolls a bit, descending and then climbing through the forest. The road and trail join at the Akamina Pass trailhead, and the groomed ski trail follows the road for the final 0.8-km descent to Cameron Lake.

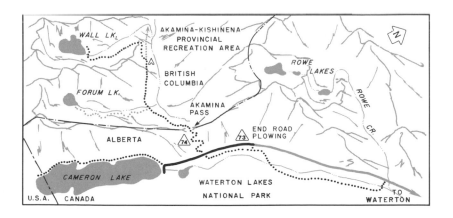

Experienced skiers may continue on, heading up the lake to reach the United States at the far end. If the ice is thin, follow the lakeshore trail along the north side of the lake for 2 km to a small, picturesque peninsula. Do not approach the steep cliffs at the end of the lake; they are very avalanche prone.

74 Wall Lake

Round trip: 14.6 km (9 mi)
Elevation gain: 251 meters (823 ft)
High point: 1890 meters (6201 ft)
Rating: difficult

The Wall Lake tour begins in Waterton Lakes National Park in Alberta. The trail climbs to Akamina Pass, where you leave the park, cross the Continental Divide, and enter the Akamina–Kishinena Provincial Recreation Area of British Columbia.

The trip is not a technically difficult one; however, there are several narrow and very steep sections of trail where lightweight track skis could easily be broken. The trail is poorly marked, so be sure to carry a compass and a good area map (maps may be purchased at the Administration Centre in downtown Waterton Park).

Access: Drive to the Waterton townsite, then head up the Akamina Parkway for 13 km to the gate at Little Prairie Picnic Shelter. Park here (elevation 1639 meters). **(See map on page 249.)**

The Tour: Follow either the Cameron Lake Ski Trail or the main road for 1.6 km to the Akamina Pass trailhead.

The Akamina Pass Trail follows the route of an old wagon road built in the late 1800s. It is wide for a trail, but narrow for a road. The trail begins by climbing steeply up the forest hillside for the first kilometer. At Akamina Pass the trail levels briefly, then heads down into British Columbia. After 1.3 km of delightful descent, the trail divides. The left fork climbs to the Recreation Area headquarters (closed for the winter), Forum Falls, and Forum Lake.

Continue straight down the valley for another 0.4 km, passing a camp area just before reaching the Wall Lake Trail intersection. Head left on the narrow trail and contour around the forested hill-

Skiing in Wall Creek valley near Wall Lake

side to another intersection. Go straight here, ignoring the sign that points up the steep hill to the left.

The lake is reached at 5.7 km from the Cameron Lake Road. Watch for avalanches near Wall Lake.

USEFUL ADDRESSES

The Parks

Superintendent
Glacier National Park
West Glacier, MT 59901
Phone: (406) 888-5441
TDD: (406) 888-5790

Superintendent
Waterton Lakes National Park
Waterton Park, AB T0K 2M0
Phone: (403) 859-2224

Flathead National Forest
1935 Third Avenue East
Kalispell, MT 59901
Phone: (406) 775-5401

Lodging

Alberta Tourism
Phone: (800) 661-1222

Apgar Village Lodge
P.O. Box 398
West Glacier, MT 59936
(406) 888-5363

Brownies Grocery and Hostel
P.O. Box 229
East Glacier Park, MT 59434
Phone: (406) 226-4426

Glacier Highland
P.O. Box 397
West Glacier, MT 59936
(406) 888-5427

Glacier Park, Inc.
(mid-October to May)
Dial Tower
Phoenix, AZ 85077-0928

Glacier Park, Inc.
(May to mid-October)
East Glacier Park, MT 59434-0147
Phone: (406) 226-5551 (U.S.)
(403) 236-3400 (Canada)

Izaak Walton Inn
P.O. Box 653
Essex, MT 59916
Phone: (406) 888-5700

North Fork Hostel
Box 1
Polebridge, MT 59928
Phone: (406) 888-5241

St. Mary Lodge
St. Mary, MT 59417
(406) 732-4431

Waterton Chamber of
    Commerce
Waterton Park, AB T0K 2M0
Phone: (403) 859-2203

Horseback Riding

Alpine Stables
P.O. Box 53
Waterton Park, AB T0K 2M0
Phone: (403) 859-2462

Glacier Park Outfitters
(mid-September to mid-May)
8320 Hazel Avenue
Orangevale, CA 95662
Phone: (916) 988-3765

Glacier Park Outfitters
(mid-May to mid-September)
Many Glacier Stable
P.O. Box 295
Babb, MT 59411
Phone: (406) 732-5597

Guides

Glacier Wilderness Guides
P.O. Box 535
West Glacier, MT 59936
Phone: (800) 521-RAFT

INDEX

addresses, useful 252
Akamina Lake 180
Akamina Parkway 178
Akamina Pass 210
Akamina–Kishinena Provincial
    Recreation Area 199, 250
Alberta Tourism 19
Alderson Lake 197
Amtrak 14, 98, 216
Apgar 35
Apgar Lookout 40
Apikuni Falls 149
Arrow Lake 49
Aster Falls 100
Autumn Creek Trail 233
Avalanche Lake 51

Babb 135, 147
backpacking 22–23
Baring Falls 129
Bauerman Creek 207
Bauerman Creek Trail 189
Bauerman Creek Valley 207
bears 26–31, 215
Bears Hump 179
Belly River 136, 160, 165, 180
Bertha Falls 181
Bertha Falls, Lower 179
Bertha Lake 181
Bertha Lake Trail 184
bicycling 23–24
Big Prairie 225
Blakiston Creek Trail 189
Blakiston Falls 180
boating 24–25
Bosporus Trail 201
Boulder Pass 174
Boulder Pass Trail 82, 174
Bowman Lake 76, 85, 227

Brown Pass 174
Buffalo Paddocks 178
Bullhead Lake 161, 243

Camas Road 220
Cameron Lake 197
Cameron Lake Ski Trail 248
Cameron Lakeshore 180
campgrounds 17–19
Carthew Pass 197
Carthew–Alderson Traverse 197
chalets 20
Chief Mountain International
    Highway 136
Cobalt Lake 105
Cracker Lake 150
Crandell Lake 178, 179
Crandell Lake Loop 203
Crypt Lake 185
Cut Bank 114
Cut Bank (bicycling) 118

Dawson Pass Loop 108
day hiking 21

East Glacier Park 98, 235
Elizabeth Lake 160, 163, 166
Essex 90, 229

Falls Hike, The 128
Fifty Mountain 163
Firebrand Pass 111
Fish Creek Campground 221
Fishercap Lake 149, 160, 244
fishing 24
Forum Lake 199
Francis, Lake 174

Garden Wall, The 144

geology 11–13
Glacier Park, Inc. 19
Glacier Park Outfitters 20
Goat Haunt 168
Goat Haunt Overlook 171
Goat Lake 187
Goat Lake Trail 190, 208
Going-To-The-Sun Road 66, 217
Going-to-the-Sun Road 37, 139
Granite Park 144, 165
Granite Park Chalet 20, 160
Grinnell Glacier 153
Grinnell Lake 152, 245
Grinnell Lake, Upper 155
Gunsight Lake 129
Gunsight Pass 46, 131

Helen Lake 167
Hidden Lake 141
Hidden Meadow 76
Hidden Meadow Trail 64
Highline Trail 144, 165
hiking, day 21–22
hiking, overnight 22
history 13–14
Hole-in-the-Wall 174
horseback riding 25
hostels 19
hotels 19
Howe Lake 40, 63
Howe Ridge 50, 63
Huckleberry Lookout 65
Huckleberry Mountain Nature
    Loop 39

Iceberg Lake 155, 159
Inside North Fork Road 62, 221, 228
International Peace Park 10
Izaak Walton Inn 229

Janet, Lake 176
Johns Lake Trail 68
Josephine, Lake 149, 152, 154, 245

Kintla Lake 82, 87
Kootenai Lakes 172

Lake McDonald Trail 53
laundry 19
Lewis Overthrust 12, 137
Lincoln Lake 67
Lineham Falls 191
Lineham Lakes 191, 195
Lineham Ridge 195
Linnet Lake Loop 179
Logan Pass 71, 139
Logging Lake Trail 55

Many Glacier 147
Marias Pass 233
McDonald, Lake 35
McGee Meadow Loop 219
Middle Fork Ride 57
motels 19
Mount Brown Lookout 42
mountain lions 31

No Name Lake 108
North Boundary Trail 184
North Fork Flathead River 61
North Fork Loop 61
North Fork Road 64
North Lake McDonald Road 59
Northern Circle, The 162
Numa Ridge Lookout 78
Nyack–Coal Creek Wilderness
    Camping Zone 94

Oldman Lake 108
Ole Creek 91
Ole Creek Trail 231
Otokomi Lake 126

Paradise Point 100
phone numbers, useful 252
Polebridge 64, 73, 223
Preston Park 133

Ptarmigan Falls 149, 156, 159
Ptarmigan Lake 159
Ptarmigan Tunnel 158, 163

Quartz Lakes Loop 80

Rainbow Falls 172, 184
Rainbow Falls Trail 176
Red Eagle Lake 123, 239
Red Rock Canyon 178, 180, 188,
    189
Red Rock Parkway 178, 207
Redrock Falls 149
Redrock Lake 149, 161, 244
Rocky Point 40
Rowe Lake, Upper 195
Rowe Lakes 193
Running Eagle Falls 100

Sacred Dancing Cascade Loop 47
Scalplock Mountain Lookout 91
Scenic Point 101
showers 19
Siyeh Bend 132
Siyeh Pass 132
Snowshoe Trail 207
Snyder Lakes 42
Sperry Chalet 20, 44, 131
Sperry Glacier 46
St. Mary 120, 238
St. Mary Falls 123, 129
St. Mary Lake 241
St. Mary to Waterton Park (bicy-
    cling) 134
Stoney Indian Pass 163

Sun Point 123
Sunrift Gorge 123, 129, 132
Swiftcurrent Lake 149, 154
Swiftcurrent Pass 160, 165
Swiftcurrent Pass Trail 156, 159
Swiftcurrent Trail 243

telephone numbers, useful 252
Townsite Trail 179
Trail of the Cedars 39
trains 14
Triple Divide Pass 115
Trout Lake 49
Twin Falls 101
Twin Lakes Loop 189
Two Medicine area 97
Two Medicine Lake 235
Two Medicine Lake Circuit 102

Upper Two Medicine Lake 107,
    108

Virginia Falls 129

Wall Lake 199, 209, 250
Walton 90, 230
Waterton Lakes National Park 176
Waterton Lakeshore Trail 170,
    176, 182
Waterton Park, town of 139
Waterton townsite 247
weather 16–17
West Glacier 35, 216
winter season 212, 212–215
Wishbone (Bosporus) Trail 201

About the authors:

VICKY SPRING and TOM KIRKENDALL are both experienced outdoor people and enthusiastic skiers. The couple travel the hills in summer as hikers, backpackers and cyclists on mountain bikes; when the snow falls, they pin on cross-country skis and keep on exploring. Both Tom and Vicky studied at the Brooks Institute of Photography in Santa Barbara, California, and are now building their careers together as outdoor photographers and guidebook authors.

Vicky and Tom are the authors of *Bicycling the Pacific Coast* and *Cross-Country Ski Tours of Washington's North Cascades* and *Washington's Cascades and Olympics*. Tom is author/photographer of *Mountain Bike Adventures in Washington's North Cascades & Puget Sound Basin* and *in Washington's South Cascades & Olympics*, all published by The Mountaineers.